This book is dedicated to my Lord Jesus Christ
whose love will always prove to be better than life.

To my amazing wife, Faith,
who always encourages me toward Christ.

To my parents, Johnny and Tina Zacchio,
who discipled me from a young age
and always showed me who Jesus is.

THIS REASONABLE RESPONSE:

A SIXTY-DAY JOURNEY GROWING AS A WORSHIPER OF GOD

By Johnny Zacchio Jr.

Published by Contented Life Publishing

E-mail: jzacchio@gmail.com

ISBN: 978-0-578-52406-1

Internal layout by Ulrika Towgood
Cover design by Ashley Garcia
Edited by Faith Collier, Miriam Rogers

Printed in United States of America

DAY 1

WHAT THE FATHER SEEKS

> *"The hour is coming, and now is, when the true worshipers will worship the Father in spirit and truth; for the Father is seeking such to worship Him."* **–John 4:23**

Have you ever sought something? You seek the things that are important or valuable to you. I think today in our modern culture, the things I look for the most are one of these three things: my keys, my phone, and my wallet. I lose one of those, I feel like I can't even leave the house. We seek things out until we find what we are looking for. Why? Because they're important to us. Valuable to us.

Did you know that God the Father is seeking something? If the God of all the universe is seeking something, it must mean it's pretty important to Him. I mean, think about this. He's God. He's self-sufficient. Self-existent. All-powerful. Created the stars by the breath of His mouth. He doesn't *need* anything, but yet He's seeking something. What does Jesus tell the Samaritan woman here in John 4 that He is seeking? He's seeking true worshipers.

True worship is important to God. If you are a Christ follower, this should be what is most important to you in all of life. We've limited worship to the twenty-five to thirty minutes on Sunday mornings before the pastor's sermon, but that's not necessarily true worship. We worship God with music, but music is not worship at its very core. Jesus is speaking of something so much deeper than what we would normally think of when we hear the word *worship*. He's speaking of a life lived in response to God. True worship comes down to the matter of the heart, and what is reigning supreme in our lives. What should characterize us as Christians, as we live our lives for God, should be that we are called "true worshiper."

Here's the question for us: Does this matter to us above everything we aspire to be? Out of the list of goals we have in life, is this at the top?

It should be. This is the purpose for which we were created, and the purpose for which we were saved. It matters to God; does it matter to you? The amazing thing is that God, by His Spirit, is committed to transforming us into just that—a true worshiper of Him.

"Blest Father of glory, we worship:
Thy greatness surpasses our praise;
We bless Thee Thy Spirit within us
Gives pow'r to these heavenly lays."
Edward Arthur

DAY 2

LET'S BE REASONABLE

"I beseech you therefore, brethren, by the mercies of God, that you present your bodies a living sacrifice, holy, acceptable to God, which is your reasonable service." **–Romans 12:1**

Worship is our response, both personal and corporate, to Who God is, and what He's done with our will, actions, and affections. In Romans 12, the apostle Paul is telling us that our response of worship to God should be reasonable. But why is this response reasonable? There are many of things in life that we would say are reasonable. When I was little, I hated when my mom would tell me to clean my room. It was a very reasonable thing for me to clean my room, due to the fact that my parents were nice enough to let me live in a beautiful, comfortable home, provide for my every need, and show me nothing but love. I soon realized that maybe cleaning my room, or helping around the house, was pretty reasonable. Paul begins this verse with "I beseech (beg) you therefore, brethren, by the **mercies of God**." He is saying that this response is to be in light of all of God's mercies! The first eleven chapters of the book of Romans right before this verse in chapter 12 were an amazing explanation and breakdown of the glorious gospel of God that was given through Jesus Christ.

The fact that the creator God of all the universe became a Man, and came to us in spite of man's disobedience, sin, and rebellion against Him; the fact that He became poor, became a curse for our sakes, taking a criminal's death on a wooden cross, and rose again three days later in victory, sealing our justification, giving us freedom from the grip of sin, and granting us eternity with Him; it is in light of *these* mercies that I respond to God, and this is what makes my response to God reasonable. When we come to a right understanding of the gospel, what Jesus has done for us and His marvelous grace toward us, we cannot help but be compelled to respond to God in worship. Have you taken the time to really think about and know the love of God? Have you become desensitized to it? Has the reality of the gospel gripped your heart? If you haven't taken the time, and you don't know God, respond to God now, open your heart and receive His gift of salvation. If you are already a child of God, may you never lose the wonder of His mercies.

"Lord, You are the only One who offered
Yourself without reluctance unto God;
Full obedience to the Father given,
Absolute, You sacrificed Your all.
As this One, You're dwelling in my spirit;
Moving, spreading outward day by day.
There's a whisper of Amen within me
In response to all that You would say."
Unknown

DAY 3

GOD'S WAY

> *"God is Spirit, and those who worship Him must worship in spirit and truth."* **–John 4:24**

I know in my own life that I want things to be done my way. What is natural for us as humans is for self to be on the throne of our heart. If we call ourselves people of God, that selfish mindset is no longer to be embraced. When it comes to true Christian worship, worship needs to be done, not my way, but God's way. Not on my terms, but on God's terms. A lot of times we want to worship God when it's convenient for us, or we allow our emotions to control our worship. But Jesus gives us a different perspective in John 4:24. In this verse, the Samaritan woman, or as I like to call her, "the woman with the water pot and the worship problem," comes to the well where Jesus was sitting, and she has a life-altering encounter.

Jesus lovingly takes the conversation from physical water to living water; from her husband to her five husbands and her present sinful lifestyle—all to engage her heart and bring her into the knowledge of Himself. The whole conversation was really about worship and Jesus revealing her worship problem found in the crevices of her heart. He tells her that worship of God cannot be confined to a location, and He tells her that true worshipers worship in *spirit* and in *truth*. Jesus lays it out so simply. We must worship God in spirit; worship springing from a sincere heart before God. Because the Spirit of God has regenerated us and made our spirits come to life, we can now worship God with sincerity of heart that flows from the inner person. This is worship focused on spiritual realities rather than outward cleansing, rituals, and sacrifices. We must worship God in truth; worship aligned with the truth of the Word of God. Our worship always needs to be guided by how God reveals Himself in His written Word, and ultimately how He reveals Himself through the Living Word. Jesus realigned this woman's understanding of worship; and to be all God has called us to be, our understanding must be aligned, as well. Jesus transformed her life, and as a result, others' lives were transformed, as well. Today, pray for God's Spirit to bring you back to sincere worship of Him. Pray for Him to align your worship with the truth that is revealed in the Scriptures. Realign your heart with God's heart. Worship Him the way He prescribes. His way is always better and brings lasting change!

"In spirit and in truth, O Lord,
We meet to worship here;
As taught by Christ, the Son of God,
We now in Him draw near."
Henry S. Cutler

DAY 4

IT NEVER STOPS

> *"... that you present your bodies a living sacrifice, holy, acceptable to God, which is your reasonable service."* **–Romans 12:1**

God is our ultimate authority, and He defines and guides us in true worship. This is incredibly foundational if we're to grow in our walk with Jesus. So what is our reasonable response supposed to look like? In light of all God has done for us in Jesus Christ, and His indescribable love toward us, how do we respond? Well, in this verse, the apostle Paul answers that question and points out that first, our worship always begins with presentation. He tells us that we must present our bodies to God. One way I've heard this presentation summed up is *my body for God's glory*. God's main desire for our worship is not that we give Him our money, our talents, or our singing in church. If you really want to be a true worshiper of God, you have to realize that all God wants is *you*—*all* of you!

Secondly, Paul tells us this reasonable response is supposed to be a living sacrifice; a realization that your life is not your own but is to be lived for another. Check out the words *living sacrifice*. Usually, sacrifices in the Old Testament were supposed to be dead sacrifices offered to God. But now in the new covenant, our offering to God is to be living sacrifices. This is very significant as it points out God's heart for a life of worship. When does worship stop? It never stops. Worship is not merely a song that is sung, but a life that is lived. This is what our worship must look like. God desires that we be men and women who live our lives dying to our own desires and wants; and instead, living moment by moment surrendered to the will of our Master. Ask yourself, have you devoted your life in full surrender to Jesus? What specific area of life have you not surrendered? True worship takes place when you come to this place of brokenness and sacrifice in light of all that Christ has done for you. We sing in church, "I surrender all," but is this reality? I challenge you, every morning before you leave your house, or before you get on with your day, pray Romans 12:1-2 into your life and present yourself to God. Watch God work wonderful things in you and through you as you continually renew your commitment to Him.

"Oh, save me from self-seeking,
Lord, Let me not be my own;
A living sacrifice I come,
Lord, keep me Thine alone."
A.B. Simpson

DAY 5

LORD, HELP ME!

> *"Then she came and worshiped Him, saying, 'Lord, help me!'"*
> **–Matthew 15:25**

Have you ever viewed desperation and dependence as worship? Apparently, Jesus did. This woman came to a place in her life where the only words she was able to muster up were, "Lord, help me!" And that simple expression was sweet worship to Jesus. Jesus was far along in His public ministry by this point. His fame has been spreading throughout Jerusalem, and many have been impacted by Him. He's been teaching multitudes, leading His disciples, healing the broken that come in His path both physically and spiritually. As Jesus is going in to Gentile territory, He encounters this Syrophoenician woman, a Gentile, in desperate need of help. She begs for mercy from Jesus, and a healing work, because her daughter is severely demon-possessed. Can you imagine the pain, anxiety and fear she is experiencing in this moment? Her daughter, the one she raised, the one she loves so dearly, is possessed by a demon. No doubt her daughter was experiencing attacks internally, and we can only imagine that this affliction can be incredibly difficult for her mother who's trying her best to figure things out, but she has nowhere to turn. She recognizes her need, so she turns to Jesus in desperation, and with full dependence. At first Jesus keeps silent and doesn't attend to her need, but perhaps this was a test of her faith. Then when she responds in full dependence and goes from calling Jesus "Son of David" to "Lord," He responds and meets her need, and her daughter is healed.

You and I were at this place. Nothing to offer, drowning in the pain and guilt of our own sin, trapped with no way out, on our way to destruction and judgment (Ephesians 2:1-6). But as we recognized our great need for a Savior and turned to Jesus, realizing that His blood shed on the cross was the only way of escape, He reached down and made us alive, performing what I could not myself. Have you come to this place in your own Christian life, where you are brought to your knees in such brokenness, and all you are able to say is, "Lord, help me"? This is pure worship, friend. Notice the phrase in this verse, "She worshiped Him saying ..." For this woman, to be broken and recognize her need for Jesus was worship.

No matter if we're going through intense suffering or if we're doing great, we should be constantly recognizing how much we need Christ and need His grace. Truly we are nothing without Him. There is no room for pride in His presence. Have you come to the place of brokenness in your own life—being broken of your own pride, self-reliance, and hardened heart that you are finally bent to the will of God and purely worshiping Him at His feet?

May we, on a daily basis, be brought to deep desperation and dependence on Jesus, and see our great need for Him. There's a great promise of blessing for those who are at this place in their heart, "Blessed are the poor in spirit, for theirs is the kingdom of heaven" (Matthew 5:3).

"I need Thee, oh I need Thee, every hour I need Thee,
oh bless me now, my Savior, I come to Thee."
Robert Lowry

DAY 6

I WILL TAKE

> *"What shall I render to the LORD for all His benefits toward me? I will take up the cup of salvation, and call upon the name of the LORD."* **–Psalm 116:12-13**

The writer of this beautiful psalm is in pure amazement and awe of God and His love and goodness. The fact that God hears his voice when he calls, is merciful to him and gracious at all times, and He is strong to save and deliver, has brought the psalmist to this place where all he can do is respond to God's goodness. God is a God who loves to bless His children in spite of who they are. Another psalm makes a similar point:

> *"Bless the LORD, O my soul; and forget not all His benefits: who forgives all your iniquities, who heals all your diseases, who redeems your life from destruction, who crowns you with loving-kindness and tender mercies..."* **–Psalm 103:2-4**

God is a God of great benefit. Look at all that God is and all that He does; it's only natural that we respond to Him. But how does the response look to this man in Psalm 116? He says, "I will take ...." Wait a minute ... shouldn't it say, "I will give ... "? No, instead He says, "I will take up the cup of salvation, and call upon the name of the LORD." In other words, "I will receive and lift up the cup of God's salvation, and simply praise His name for what He's done." Although we give and surrender our whole life as a response to God, worship also involves receiving. It pleases and blesses God when we simply receive everything He gives to us as His children. Ephesians 1 says that we've been given "every spiritual blessing in heavenly places." Just like when my Italian grandma makes me a huge plate of spaghetti to eat, what makes her most happy is when I clean my plate, or even ask for seconds!

Here are a few ways we can respond to God's goodness:

1. RECOGNIZE THAT YOU ARE NOTHING WITHOUT JESUS.

When I see myself in light of who God is, His holiness, His greatness, His power, and His mercy, I have a right view of myself. When I view myself as great and strong enough, then I can be filled with pride and not even appreciate, or have any sort of gratitude, for God's goodness.

2. REST IN HIS LOVE AND HIS BENEFITS TOWARD YOU.

God delights in His children humbly receiving His benefits. Don't think you have to do a bunch of works and religious rituals in order to earn or gain any kind of favor from God and make Him love you more. That's not the gospel. God already accepts you and delights in you; receive that blessing and walk in it. Humble yourself before that old rugged cross and hear those words, "It is finished!" as He bowed His head and took your place. It's been said, "God treated Jesus as if He's lived our sinful life, so He could treat you and me for eternity as if we've lived His perfect life." What an incredible reality in which to find ultimate rest.

3. RESPOND IN PRAISE TO GOD'S NAME FOR ALL THAT HE'S DONE FOR YOU.

Take a few moments to go through the Scriptures and count all God's promises and gifts toward you and begin to praise Him and be thankful for what He's done. And ultimately, look to the cross and that empty tomb. Your soul was saved, and you were washed clean of all your sin and shame, you've been given a new name and a new identity. "Oh, give thanks to the LORD for He is good! For His mercy endures forever" (Psalm 136:1).

"My sin—oh, the bliss
of this glorious thought—
My sin, not in part, but the whole,
Is nailed to the Cross,
and I bear it no more;
Praise the Lord, praise the Lord,
O my soul!"
Horatio Spafford

DAY 7

OH, TO BE LIKE YOU

> *"And do not be conformed to this world, but be transformed by the renewing of your mind, that you may prove what is that good and acceptable and perfect will of God."* **–Romans 12:2**

When I was really young, I remember my dad telling me, "Show me who your friends are, and I'll show you who you are." There's a lot of truth to that statement. The longer you are friends with someone, the closer of a relationship you have with them, the more you start to imitate them. You can start to react like them, view life like them, make the same jokes and say certain things the way they say them. It's no wonder that even in the short time that my wife and I have been married, we've started to become like each other that much more. Similarly, we become like what or who we worship.

Every person on earth, whether a believer in Christ or not, is a worshiper. Everyone worships someone or something. If someone's worship is redirected away from God, and they begin to find their ultimate source of meaning, fulfillment, and joy in anything or anyone other than God, they are engaging in idolatry. We were put on earth to worship and adore the true and living God! The One who created all things and sent His only Son to the world so that His creation might be saved. He's worthy of our worship. Here's the amazing thing about our worship; not only does it begin with presentation, as the apostle Paul pointed out in Romans 12:1, but as we see here, worship always results in transformation.

As we draw near to Jesus and worship Him, and our relationship and love for Him deepens, you know what happens? His Holy Spirit will transform us into the image of Jesus Christ. The more we worship Jesus, the more our hearts become aligned with His and the more His characteristics will manifest in our lives. This is why having a time and place where we daily meet with God and spend quality time in His Word, the Bible, is so essential. This is why it's so important that we don't neglect that place of prayer and drawing near to God by calling upon His name. There's a promise in the scriptures, "Draw near to God and He will draw near to you" (James 4:8). And as God draws near to you, the more His light will reveal impurity and sin in your heart and His Spirit will begin to cleanse you.

The very next part of James 4:8 says, "Cleanse your hands, you sinners; and purify your hearts, you double minded." Our devotion to God, our continual worship of Him in every area of life, will have lasting results. We'll become transformed. The fragrance of Christ will be emanating from our lives and draw a world in such desperate need to the person of Jesus. Search your heart today. If you're not continually being transformed, the question is: Are you a worshiper of God? Or do other people or things have your attention and affection? If Jesus has your full affection, you will be transformed.

"O to be like Thee! Blessed Redeemer;
This is my constant longing and prayer;
Gladly I'll forfeit all of earth's treasures,
Jesus, Thy perfect likeness to wear."
Thomas Obediah Chrisholm

DAY 8

SACRIFICE

> *Then He said, "Take now your son, your only son Isaac, whom you love, and go to the land of Moriah, and offer him there as a burnt offering on one of the mountains of which I shall tell you."*
> **–Genesis 22:2**

Abraham was a man who loved and worshiped God until the day He died. On this day, Abraham's faith and worship of God was put to the test like never before. Up to this point, God had done a lot in Abraham's life. Abraham displayed patience and what it meant to truly wait on and trust in the Lord. One of the ways he displayed this was resolving to believe the promise of God to bring him a child. He and his wife took matters into their own hands, and they ended up having a son through a different woman. Not a good idea. God didn't honor this decision. But afterward God finally brought Abraham a son whom he named Isaac. This was an amazing day for Abraham and his wife! God's promise finally coming to pass! Oh the joy they must have experienced raising their only son. They had such deep love for this boy. They probably looked at him as the greatest blessing and gift from God they had ever received.

Now we see in this chapter, Abraham, the worshiper of God, the strong man of faith, in one of the most difficult and heart-wrenching tests he had ever been in. He is commanded to kill his only son. The test of Abraham's love and worship of God was that of obedience and sacrifice. Of course, God stopped Abraham right before he would go through with the sacrifice; God was pleased! He knew that Abraham loved God, for he would not even withhold his only son from Him. Something incredibly foundational to our worship is to understand that pure worship is sacrifice and obedience.

If you desire to grow as a worshiper of Christ, here are a few questions to ask yourself as you examine your own heart.

1. HAVE YOU GIVEN YOUR LIFE FULLY OVER TO THE AUTHORITY OF JESUS?

Jesus said, "All authority has been given unto Me in heaven and on earth" (Matthew 28:18). Jesus is Lord, but is He *your* Lord? If you do not look to God as the ultimate authority in your life and you have not submitted to Him, you are not a worshiper of Jesus.

2. WHAT DO YOU NEED TO SACRIFICE IN YOUR LIFE THAT HAS TAKEN THE PLACE OF GOD IN YOUR HEART?

Maybe God is testing you. Your faith in Him and your worship of Him will be put to the test to see if it's genuine. Search your heart for idolatry. In light of all that God has sacrificed for you, be willing to sacrifice anything to God that has gripped your heart. Maybe it's a particular sin in your life that you continually feed and hide. Maybe it's a good thing, like your family, your spouse, or your job. Jesus said if you don't love Him more than anyone or anything, you are not worthy of Him.

3. HAVE YOUR EMOTIONS BECOME YOUR LORD?

Notice in this story how after God commanded Abraham to sacrifice his own son, the Bible never tells us how he felt about it. I believe that's intentional. At this point, Abraham's feelings and emotions were irrelevant. It didn't matter how Abraham felt about it. God's desire was obedience that would glorify Him. Abraham obeyed because his emotions were not his Lord. Do not make your decision to worship God based on your emotions.

4. HAVE YOU LOST SIGHT OF THE GOSPEL?

Our worship of God should always be a response to the great message of the gospel. Jesus, with joy in His heart, submitted Himself to the will of the Father, and obeyed His command to go to the cross. What would've happened if Jesus had not obeyed that command? What if He had not sacrificed Himself? We would still be lost and dead in our sin with no hope of eternal life. Obedience and sacrifice are a big deal to God. Look to what Jesus has done and allow the gospel to motivate and enable you to live a life of obedience to God's Word. You were redeemed! We respond to that redemption with love toward God. A love toward God that resembles Christ: a response of obedience.

"Tis the plan of life, for you die to live,
One with Jesus crucified;
With the life alone to be lived through you,
Of the Risen, the Glorified."
Mary E. Maxwell

DAY 9

ETERNAL IMPACT

> *"The woman then left her waterpot, went her way into the city, and said to the men,"Come, see a Man who told me all things that I ever did. Could this be the Christ?"* **–John 4:28-29**

Here we see the woman at the well with the waterpot and the worship problem. She's had an amazing encounter with the living God and was forever changed from that day forward. Jesus' goal was to transform this woman into a true worshiper of God; after all, that is what He is ultimately seeking. All humans were created to know, love and worship God. So after Jesus talks with this woman, after He corrects her view of worship and reveals her heart, she confesses Him as the Christ, and from this point she is a true worshiper. Whereas before, her view of worship was only about a zip code, now she understands God's infinite worth, and how He should be worshiped in spirit and in truth. But what are the results of true worship?

As we worship God through everyday life, there are so many lasting results. But one of those results is that our lives will bear eternal impact for the kingdom of God. We were all destined for impact; to glorify God and point the world to Jesus during this short time that we live on the earth—but the only way this can take place is if we are worshipers of God, set apart and devoted to Him.

After this woman commits herself to Christ, in these verses in John 4, the Bible tells us that she left her waterpot. In other words, she left behind what was empty and doesn't satisfy, and went into the city to tell others about this Jesus who changed her life. The more we draw near to God with a true heart of worship, the more we experience who He is and more of His love; and therefore, the more we begin to reflect who He is and His love to the world. Your public impact in this world will be dependent upon your private worship and devotion to God. As you continue to pursue Jesus and worship Him in spirit and in truth, you are going to make a lasting, eternal impact on this earth and further the kingdom of God until He takes us home. Do you desire to impact the world with the gospel? As you deepen your worship of God, you'll begin to see Him work through you in marvelous ways.

"Channels of life are we,
Allowing God to flow!
Through us and out of us
That others life may know!"
J. G.

DAY 10

BEAUTIFUL BROKENNESS

> *"In the year that King Uzziah died, I saw the Lord sitting on a throne, high and lifted up, and the train of His robe filled the temple. So I said: 'Woe is me, for I am undone! Because I am a man of unclean lips, and I dwell in the midst of a people of unclean lips; for my eyes have seen the King, The LORD of hosts.'"* **–Isaiah 6:1, 5**

I do not believe that our worship of God can be divorced from brokenness. Worshiping God will always involve brokenness. God views our brokenness as beautiful, and even as a prerequisite to a deeper, more mature relationship with Himself. Brokenness is also useful in the kingdom of God. When we hear the word broken, we often think of the opposite—that brokenness is the opposite of anything beautiful and good. In the moment it can feel this way. Sometimes it comes as a result of some trial or hardship we are dealing with. Or it happens when our impurities rise to the surface, and we're faced with our weaknesses and our deep need. We recognize we don't have what it takes to live life, our pride is wounded, and we become, as Jesus describes, "poor in spirit." How could being poor be good? Well, what it brings forth in a person's life is anything but hideous, it's life-changing. Just as when you desire to plant something beautiful, weeds must be pulled and the soil must be broken up. But the end result is always life. Brokenness is necessary in our walk with God. It leads to greater intimacy with God and deeper worship of God. Here's how it happened for the prophet Isaiah.

1. BROKENNESS BEGAN WITH A TRAGEDY IN HIS NATION (V. 1A).

"In the year that King Uzziah died ..." King Uzziah was one of the greatest kings the nation of Israel ever had. Under his reign were times of great reform, flourishing, and strength for Israel. It was at the time of King Uzziah's death, and the resulting tragedy and trial, that God chose to break Isaiah and transform him. Trials are promised to us as God's people, but when they come God accomplishes His eternal purpose in us and through us.

2. BROKENNESS CAME AS A RESULT OF A REVELATION OF WHO GOD WAS (V. 1B).
In this time of great tragedy, God chose to reveal who He was to Isaiah, and it was magnificent, to say the least. He saw the King of all the universe in all His glory, exalted and lifted up. He saw that God was all-powerful, all-glorious, beautiful in His holiness, and preeminent. Isaiah recognized there is no god like this God; no king on earth like this King.

3. BROKENNESS RESULTED IN A RIGHT VIEW OF HIMSELF (V. 5)
A right view of God brings a right view of self. When God was revealed to Isaiah, he saw his impurities and his depravity in a way he hadn't before. When we see God, we see His greatness and His power. We see His vastness and His holiness. Then we see the gospel, and we see His justice and His mercy. We see His goodness and His love. Our response should be as Isaiah's was "Woe is me…" Brokenness happens and it should manifest itself in a right view of ourselves, a humility before God, and a confession of our sin.

4. BROKENNESS RESULTED IN RESTORATION, HEALING AND COMMISSION (V. 7).
As Isaiah was broken and without hesitation displayed humility before God, the Bible tells us that an angel flew to him with a coal from the altar, touched his mouth and cleansed him. The coal being a picture and symbol of God's cleansing power over our sin, Isaiah was forgiven, cleansed and restored. And so too, as we come humbly before God in confession and brokenness, through the cross of Christ, God washes and purges our sin for eternity. Through His resurrection we receive His victory and power over sin, and we receive His healing, and His hands put us back together. And not only did Isaiah receive forgiveness and redemption, but He received a commission. When God asks, "Whom shall I send, and who will go for Us?" (v. 8) Isaiah immediately says, "Here I am! Send me." Isaiah is sent by God to become one of the most effective prophets Israel has ever known, a man by which God would communicate to His people warning, as well as comfort and consolation.

Let's be broken daily before God and watch our worship of Him deepen —and our lives changed and used for change for His glory!

"Nothing in my hands
I bring, Simply to Thy cross I cling;
Naked, come to Thee for dress,
Helpless, look to Thee for grace:
Foul, I to the fountain fly,
Wash me, Savior, or I die."
Augustus Toplady

DAY 11

WORSHIP THROUGH SUFFERING

> *"Blessed be the God and Father of our Lord Jesus Christ, who according to His abundant mercy has begotten us again to a living hope through the resurrection of Jesus Christ from the dead, to an inheritance incorruptible and undefiled and that does not fade away, reserved in heaven for you."* **–1 Peter 1:3-4**

Everyone experiences pain. It's inevitable. But even through the suffering, we can have a proper response to God and worship Him, even when the most difficult circumstances come our way. Learning to worship God through suffering can be something that strengthens our faith, gives us endurance and glorifies Jesus. It's never easy or natural to do, but by God's grace and by God's Spirit, we can. You may or may not know this but our perspective and our response to suffering can actually be worship to God. In this passage, the apostle Peter is encouraging these believers in the very midst of their tempestuous storms to get their minds on the right thing. If our eyes are fixed upon how difficult the road is, or how miserable our trial is, we will never be able to worship God through it; and as a result, we will not become the person God has created us to be for His glory. So what's Peter's comfort in the midst of their suffering? The hope they have in the gospel. That's our great comfort in suffering, friend, the good news of salvation accomplished through the death, burial, and resurrection of Jesus Christ. Our proper response of worship to God in trials should be to rejoice in the hope we have in Christ as believers. And how can we do that? In this chapter, I believe Peter gives us 3 ways.

1. REMEMBER THE PAST.

In verses 1-5 Peter reminds these Christians, and reminds you and me, to remember our past; what Christ has already done for us! He's begotten us again to a living hope through the resurrection of Jesus from the dead. We've been given an eternal, undefiled inheritance, and it's reserved in heaven for us, kept by God's power. What an incredible hope we have through what Christ has done for us. If you feel there's nothing good going on in your life right now, hope in what Christ has done for you.

2. REST IN THE PRESENT.

Peter goes on in verses 6-8 to encourage them to find rest in what God is presently doing during their suffering. Did you know that God is at work in and through your present circumstance? That's what God's Word reveals to us. The apostle Paul makes a similar point in 2 Corinthians 4:17, "For our light affliction, which is but for a moment, is working for us." Your present suffering is not meaningless, but incredibly meaningful, because as Peter points out in this section, God is sanctifying us, testing us, and making our faith more genuine. Just as when gold is placed through fire it becomes more pure, fine and beautiful, so too, God uses what He puts us through to make us more like Himself.

3. REALIZE THE FUTURE.

In verses 9-12 Peter points to the future of these believers. A promise that is sure and eternal. It's important to cultivate an eternal perspective in the midst of trials, because when we are focused on the temporal we can grow despondent and depressed.

I love what H. A. Ironside once wrote, "When everything that the eye looks upon will have vanished, we shall have Christ, we shall have heaven, we shall have the Holy Spirit, we shall have the love of the Father, we shall have communion with the people of God for all eternity, when earth's vain shadows have passed away."[1] This is your future hope. We have an eternal home not made with hands; and as every tear is wiped from our eyes, we will be looking at the face of the One who saved us and gave us life.

Let's respond to God through our suffering by rejoicing in the hope of our past, present, and future salvation.

"All the way my Savior leads me,
Cheers each winding path I tread,
Gives me grace for every trial,
Feeds me with the living bread.
Fanny Crosby

---

[1] H. A. Ironside, *Addresses on the Second Epistle to the Corinthians.* Public domain.

DAY 12

THE RESPONSE OF REVERENCE

"The fear of the LORD leads to life, and he who has it will abide in satisfaction; he will not be visited by evil." **–Proverbs 19:23**

Something that can be lost in the life of a Christian at times is the beauty of reverence before God. It could be that we've lost sight of who God is and His very presence all around us. A.W. Tozer writes, "Many persons who have been raised in our churches no longer think in terms of reverence, which seems to indicate that they doubt God's presence is there."[2] The *fear* of God in this proverb speaks of a reverence for God. And reverence can be defined as having a deep respect for someone superior. If we truly desire to be a true worshiper of God, it happens by being in a continual state of reverence before God, or having what the Proverbs call the "fear of the Lord."

Solomon says here that this fear of God, or reverence before God, is the key to all of life. True worship of God will not happen if we do not reverence God. A proper response to who God is, is to fall in reverence before His feet, seeing that He is so glorious. A beautiful example of this is when Ezekiel was caught up in a vision, witnessing the very glory and presence of God; Ezekiel said this about his experience: "This was the appearance of the likeness of the glory of the LORD. So when I saw it, I fell on my face, and I heard the voice of One speaking" (Ezekiel 1:28).

One practice that is amazing for every Christian to do is to go through the Scriptures and read about the very nature and character of God, to really think on who God is. When we finally do that, we come to find out how worthy He is of our praise and reverence. May we never lose the fear of God. May we restore the knowledge of who God is to

---

[2]Tozer, A. W. "THE NEED FOR REVERENCE - Sermon Index." SermonIndex Audio Sermons, 1980, www.sermonindex.net/modules/articles/index.php?view=article&aid=4723.

our lives, continually live with the awareness of His presence, and just like Ezekiel, be so amazed that we cannot help but be bent low toward Christ, ready to fully submit, fully worship, and live life for Him. God in His grace and mercy will allow us to be broken before Him that we may gain a right view of Him, and a right view of ourselves, and have reverence be restored to our everyday lives. It's only then, according to this proverb, that we will be living a fully satisfied life. Do you desire to abide in satisfaction? Live in the fear of God.

"Holy, holy, holy! Lord God Almighty!
All Thy works shall praise Thy name,
In earth and sky and sea;
Holy, holy, holy! Merciful and mighty!
God in three Persons, blessed Trinity!"
Reginald Heber

DAY 13

OUR WORSHIP AND SINGING

Part 1

> *"Oh, sing to the LORD a new song! For He has done marvelous things; His right hand and His holy arm have gained Him the victory."* **–Psalm 98:1**

In light of who God is and all the wonderful things He has done, singing should be the natural by-product in every Christian's life. When speaking of our worship of God, singing is one of the primary ways that we as Christians worship. Music and singing aren't worship at its very core as many today might think, but it is an important way that we respond to God. God has invented the voice to be used to glorify Himself; not only to speak forth His word, but also to sing forth His praises. God commands us to sing, and for good reason! Singing magnifies the beauty and greatness of God in a special way. The way we truly walk with Jesus is by walking in the Spirit. When walking in the Spirit, singing should be a natural overflow of the believer's life, as well. In Ephesians chapter 5, the apostle Paul points out that one of the things that shows the Spirit is at work in a person's life is "speaking to one another in psalms and hymns and spiritual songs, singing and making melody in your heart to the Lord" (v. 19). I love the attitude of the psalmist in the psalm quoted above. He's giving this plea to sing to the Lord a new song, and I love his reason: "For He has done marvelous things." When was the last time you took the time to think on the marvelous works of God? If you do, you can't help but just sing forth God's praises. The Spirit within you produces a melody in your heart. Just goes to show that words sometimes are just not enough.

Even if singing isn't necessarily your "thing," or you probably think your voice is the kind that no one would care to listen to, singing is incredibly important for your worship of God. Not only because God commands it, which should be enough, but because it engages the heart and the emotions so that you don't just think and know good things about God but you express and respond with your feelings toward God. We're not only called to love the LORD our God with all our *mind*, but also with all our *heart* (Matthew 22:37).

Pastor John Piper puts it this way, "Singing is the Christian's way of saying: God is so great that thinking will not suffice, there must be deep feeling; and talking will not suffice, there must be singing."[3] So think upon the goodness of God and His marvelous works, and ask Him to fill you with His Holy Spirit, and allow Him to fill you with a melody that can be used to respond to all He's done. As His praise is continually on your mouth, you will, even through the most difficult of times, glorify God! "I will remember my song in the night; I will meditate with my heart, and my spirit ponders" (Psalm 77:6 NASB).

"I have a song I love to sing,
Since I have been redeemed,
Of my Redeemer, Savior, King—
Since I have been redeemed."
Edwin Othello Excell

---

3 "Singing and Making Melody to the Lord." Desiring God, 21 July 2018, www.desiringgod.org/messages/singing-and-making-melody-to-the-lord

DAY 14

OUR WORSHIP AND SINGING Part 2

> *"Then it shall be, when many evils and troubles have come upon them, that this song will testify against them as a witness; for it will not be forgotten in the mouths of their descendants."*
> **–Deuteronomy 31:21**

Music and singing are incredible tools and are used by God to help us remember truth about who He is. I think back to when I was a child and how I learned my ABC's. Like most of us, I sang them! When I was a high school student and I was studying for my biology test, I crafted this beautiful medley of vocabulary words (still did poorly on the test, I was an awful test taker) but nonetheless it helped me remember the vocabulary.

Bob Kauflin, in his book, *Worship Matters*, points out that music was created by God so that we, His people, can remember His truth.[4] Music will oftentimes bring the truth we know about God contained in our minds down to our hearts, and will result in an overflow to our lips, and through our lives. Music is a lot more powerful than we give it credit for. It is evident that God's purpose for music has been tainted and distorted by our wicked human hearts. God's purpose always was and always will be that we, as humans, get to know Him; I mean, truly *know* Him. To pursue Him by learning His truth, knowing His heart, and obeying His word. So God created music so that we would do just this.

You ever wonder why people gather in a building to sing songs to God? People of the world can look on and think this is just plain weird! But there's a powerful thing that's happening. We gather as His church every week and sing to remind each other and remember the truth of the gospel, and the truth of His word—for the end result of having

4 "...With Music...(Part One: What Kind?)." *Worship Matters: Leading Others to Encounter the Greatness of God* by Bob Kauflin, Crossway Books, 2008, p. 99.

a deeper knowledge of Him, and a life that bears fruit! Don't forsake that time! The great reformer and theologian Martin Luther would have His congregation learn truth about God by singing hymns! It was Martin Luther who said, "Next to the Word of God, the noble art of music is the greatest treasure in the world." Next time you read the Word of God, and think upon the truths that are written, the promises that are revealed; respond to those very things with the melody God places in your heart. Go to your local church, gather with the believers, and respond to who God is, and what He's done, "that you may with one mind and with one mouth glorify the God and Father of our Lord Jesus Christ" (Romans 15:6).

"O praise ye the Lord! All things that give sound;
Each jubilant chord re-echo around;
Loud organs, His glory forth tell in deep tone,
And sweet harp, the story of what He hath done."
H. W. Baker

DAY 15

FOREVER THANKFUL

> *"Therefore by Him let us continually offer the sacrifice of praise to God, that is, the fruit of our lips, giving thanks to His name."*
> **–Hebrews 13:15**

Being thankful can sometimes be difficult to do. We are people who have access to excess, and we can lose sight of what's important, and therefore cultivate an attitude of being ungrateful. I remember a recent birthday I had, opening a gift from a family member and thinking in my ungrateful wicked heart, "That's all? Is there anything else?" Even in that small moment on my birthday, I lost sight of what matters most, and I allowed myself to be discontented and ungrateful. We as God's people never, ever, ever have a reason to be ungrateful or unthankful. The writer of Hebrews gives us some instruction on what it means to be thankful, and how we can cultivate an attitude of worship by being thankful; and as a result, live lives that are filled with God's joy, which gives us God's strength.

1. "THEREFORE BY HIM ..."

Being thankful always needs to start with "by Him." It's this idea that thankfulness is only a by- product of God's work within me. It is not natural for us to be thankful people. If you have an attitude of being ungrateful, ask for God's enabling, and His power to work in you a heart of gratitude.

2. "LET US CONTINUALLY OFFER ..."

Being thankful before God is something that we can actually do by God's strength, but not only that, it's something that we can *continually* do by Gods strength. It's something that can be consistent in our life. Why? Because we have a God who is unchanging, and is *continually* present in our lives, working and making us more like Christ. We have a God who is *continually* gracious and merciful toward us as sinners. We can *continually* offer thanksgiving to our great God.

3. "A SACRIFICE OF PRAISE TO GOD ..."

Being thankful is a sacrifice of praise. As selfish humans, being thankful never comes naturally to us; it takes a great deal of dying to self in order for this attitude to manifest in our lives. It takes our surrender; our will being submitted to His.

4. "THAT IS, THE FRUIT OF OUR LIPS, GIVING THANKS TO HIS NAME."

Notice this thankful attitude should be the *fruit of our lips*. When we know who God is—*giving thanks to His name*—and we consider the amazing and wondrous works that He has done for us, what naturally starts to happen is our hearts overflow and our lips can't help but speak the praise of God. Fruit is simply a natural by-product of a tree being firmly rooted in healthy soil; and so too, the fruit of our lips can be filled with thanksgiving as we abide in Christ. Immerse yourself and get your roots deeply planted in the Scriptures so that the fruit of your lips and your life will be praise that brings glory to God!

"Give thanks to God the Lord;
upon His name now call.
Make known among the people on earth
what He has done for all.
Sing praise to Him, now sing;
His wondrous acts proclaim.
Rejoice, all you who seek the Lord;
come glory in His Name."
Susan H. Peterson (Public domain)

DAY 16

WORSHIP AND THE WORD OF CHRIST

Part 1

> *"Let the word of Christ dwell in you richly, in all wisdom, teaching and admonishing one another in psalms and hymns and spiritual songs, singing with grace in your hearts to the Lord."* **—Colossians 3:16**

The apostle Paul was passionate about the word of Christ. Most commentators believe this is referring to the word about Christ; in other words, the gospel message. This glorious message is central to the entirety of God's Word from beginning to end. If we desire to grow as worshipers of God, our growth can never happen apart from the Word of God, the Bible. Our worship of God can never be divorced from the Word of God.

In this section of Scripture, Paul is pointing out why it's so essential for our own growth to have the word of Christ dwelling in us *richly*. For good reason, because it's in the Word of God that we find all things that pertain to life and godliness (2 Peter 1:3). It's in the Word of God that we understand every aspect of the heart and mind of God (Psalm 119:104). It's in the Word of God that we are sanctified and made holy (John 17:17). It's in the Word of God that we find true joy (Psalm 119:162). It's the Word of God being the authority in our lives that qualifies us as true worshipers of God (John 4:23). It's the Word of God that truly leads us to know the God of the Word, the living Word, Jesus Christ (John 1:1,14).

Paul's challenge to us is to have the word of Christ dwelling in us richly. If this happens, our hearts begin to overflow with God's praise into the lives of those around us, resulting in lasting impact. Pastor and author Warren Wiersbe comments, "If God's word is not in our hearts, we cannot sing from our hearts. This shows how important it is to know the word of God for it enriches our public and private worship."[5] All worship is a response, and when God's word is in our hearts and dwelling within us on a daily basis, our response to God is life-altering, genuine, and grounded in truth. So today, don't just ask yourself, "When can I read my Bible today?" Ask yourself, "How can I let God's Word dwell in me richly today?" There is definitely a difference. Ask God to work in you a deeper passion and delight in the Word of God, and watch God establish you like "a tree planted by rivers of water, that brings forth fruit in its season, whose leaf also shall not wither; and whatever he does shall prosper" (Psalm 1:3).

"Jesus, O living Word of God,
Wash me and cleanse me with Your blood
So You can speak to me.
Just let me hear Your words of grace,
Just let me see Your radiant face,
Beholding constantly."
Unknown

---

5 "All Dressed Up and Someplace to Go." *Be Complete* by Warren W. Wiersbe, Victor Bks., 1986, p. 119.

DAY 17

WORSHIP AND THE WORD OF CHRIST Part 2

> *"... teaching and admonishing one another in psalms and hymns and spiritual songs, singing with grace in your hearts to the Lord."* **–Colossians 3:16**

Not only does God's word that's at work within us cause us to respond to God with songs of praise toward Him, but it also causes us to respond to God by edifying or building up the people around us. *Teaching and admonishing one another.* Author and worship leader Bob Kauflin wrote, "God is just as interested in how we treat others as He is in our songs of praise. Actually he's *more* interested."[6] Again, worship is a life that we live. This implies that this life is supposed to be devoted to these two things: to love God with all our hearts, and to love our neighbor as ourselves (Matthew 22:37). These are the two greatest commandments, the main things that Jesus requires of us; the main thing that should be our focus. I think sometimes the problem can be the second part of that commandment. We think God is only pleased with our songs to Him, and He is when expressed from a sincere heart. But He's also pleased by the way we love and treat others.

The apostle John puts it this way, "If someone says 'I love God,' and hates his brother, he is a liar" (1 John 4:20). If we truly love God, we will love others. When the love of Christ is worked in us, His love compels us to serve and love those around us. We will begin to reflect the glorious gospel of God shown through Jesus Christ. This is a direct result of the Word of God in a person's life. As we allow God's word to dwell in us richly, and work in us, and we genuinely love those around

---

6 "Always People." *Worship Matters: Leading Others to Encounter the Greatness of God*, by Bob Kauflin, Crossway Books, 2008, p. 216

us, we shed light on the cross and point people's focus and attention to our Savior, who loved us and served us through laying down His life on the cross. God desires that as His word is dwelling in us richly, that we would build up and serve those around us. May we as the body of Christ allow God's word to pour into us continually and overflow into the lives of those we encounter, so that with Jesus as our cornerstone, we can continually be those living stones which "are being built up a spiritual house, a holy priesthood, to offer up spiritual sacrifices acceptable to God through Jesus Christ" (1 Peter 2:5).

"Love is the golden chain that binds;
The saints Thy grace thus prove.
And he is glory's heir that finds
His bosom glow with love."
Joseph Swain

DAY 18

IN YOUR PRESENCE

"You will show me the path of life; in Your presence is fullness of joy; at Your right hand are pleasures forevermore." **–Psalm 16:11**

David here understands that there is nothing in the whole world like being in the presence of God. In God's presence real pleasure, freedom, love, and true joy is found. As we turn our hearts to worship God, one thing we have to understand is that we do so in the presence of God. God's presence is real and can be known and experienced. We are always in the presence of God, of course, because God is everywhere at once, and even dwelling within us as His people. As the people of God, on a daily basis, we should be diligent to encounter the living God through turning our attention to His presence—continually having that awareness. It's not simply a "feeling" or an emotional experience, it's a continual mindset that focuses on the fact that Jesus is always present, and that He desires people to know Him personally and intimately; worshiping Him in spirit and truth. So how do we pursue a greater awareness of God's presence, which leads to us encountering the living God?

1. ENCOUNTERING GOD IN HIS PRESENCE IS ONLY POSSIBLE THROUGH JESUS.
Not only is God's presence always around us, God's presence became tangible when God sent the Man Jesus Christ to the earth. He was the very presence of God upon the earth. His very name is called "God with us." And when He shed His blood upon the cross, the Bible tells us that the veil of the temple was torn in two! This picture and idea confirms that the one thing separating God's people from His presence was done away with! It's only because of Jesus and what He has done that we can come "boldly before the throne of grace" (Hebrew 4:16).

2. ENCOUNTERING GOD IN HIS PRESENCE HAPPENS THROUGH HIS WORD AND PRAYER.
There should be a continual habit of being in God's Word and being committed to prayer; two primary ways that we can encounter God.

We can continue in God's presence throughout every minute of the day talking with God, not just on Sundays. Brother Lawrence put it beautifully, "That we should establish ourselves in a sense of God's presence by continually conversing with Him. That it was a shameful thing to quit His conversation to think of trifles and fooleries."[7]

3. ENCOUNTERING GOD IN HIS PRESENCE HAPPENS WHEN WE INTERACT WITH THE CHURCH.

When Jesus left the earth, He sent the Holy Spirit to be the presence of God on the earth. The Spirit is now dwelling within the people of God. The church of Christ is the very presence of God on the earth. The body of Christ is necessary for our spiritual growth, and if we are not consistent in fellowship with others, we will not encounter God like we could if we were!

God is not reluctant to reveal Himself to us. He promises us that as we pursue Him and wait with eager expectation, His presence will be known and we will encounter the only One who can save, transform, and use us powerfully for His glory!

"In the secret of His presence
How my soul delights to hide!
Oh, how precious are the lessons
Which I learn at Jesus' side!"
Ellen Goreh

---

[7] Brother Lawrence, *The Practice of the Presence of God.* (Grand Rapids, MI: Baker Books, 1967).

DAY 19

REST IN HIS PRESENCE

> *"And He said, 'My Presence will go with you, and I will give you rest.' Then he said to Him, 'If Your Presence does not go with us, do not bring us up from here. For how then will it be known that Your people and I have found grace in Your sight, except You go with us? So we shall be separate, Your people and I, from all the people who are upon the face of the earth.'"* **–Exodus 33:14-16**

Have you ever felt like you were in desperate need of rest? In the state that both the nation of Israel and Moses himself were in, they were in desperate need of rest. This rest had to begin with restoration. Just before this, Moses had been on Mount Sinai for quite some time, alone with almighty God, receiving commandments and instructions to deliver to the nation—only to come down the mountain and find the children of Israel worshiping a golden calf. Their worship was redirected elsewhere; their hearts given over to idolatry. Tragic. God in His grace brings Moses back up to Mount Sinai to give the people a second chance. What Moses was doing was partnering with God in restoring true worship to the people. That's always when restoration begins in the heart of a person; when worship is completely directed away from self, others, and things, and back to the true and living God.

I love God's promise here in verse 14, "My Presence will go before you, and I will give you rest." Moses is seeking to lead the people the right way and allow the people to be restored, according to God's promise. True worship will take place when we begin to have renewed awareness of the presence of God in our own lives. Moses recognizes that without God being with them, going before them, there's no purpose for life, no strength, and no success in their influence on the other nations.

Friend, have you believed this promise? Have you found rest in the presence of God going before you and being with you? As you seek to be a worshiper of God, seek to enter God's rest. As you do, you will see God work powerfully in your life because you're no longer being dependent upon self, but you're being fully dependent upon God and His promise to be with you and go before you. Oftentimes throughout Scripture, when great heroes of faith were afraid, the way God assures them is not with physical tools or resources, but with His very presence. I can assure you, even though you may not "feel" like His presence is there, you can go past your feelings and recognize that we have a God who is full of promises; He's a God who cannot lie, therefore, there's no promise He can't keep. Rest in God's presence as you worship Him through whatever challenges you face today.

"A mighty fortress is our God,
A bulwark never failing;
Our helper He amid the flood
Of mortal ills prevailing."
Martin Luther

DAY 20

WHO DO YOU SAY THAT I AM?

> *"He said to them, 'But who do you say that I am?' Simon Peter answered and said, 'You are the Christ, the Son of the living God.'"* **–Matthew 16:15-16**

The apostle Paul in Philippians chapter 3 declares to the church he was writing to that His only ambition, above all else, was to know Christ. He forsook all and any accomplishment that was behind him, and pressed toward the goal of knowing Christ, because it is far better and above every pursuit in life. To know God, to know what He is like, to answer the question that was posed to Peter, "Who do *you* say that I am?" is vitally important to our worship of God. It was A. W. Tozer who famously wrote, "What comes into our minds when we think about God is the most important thing about us."[8] It's far different to simply know facts about the Savior, know theological facts about God, than it is to truly know Christ and believe what He says to be true about Himself. If we truly know Christ, having not just a head knowledge but an experiential knowledge, and if we truly take Him at His word and believe these truths revealed about Him, it will dramatically affect our life of worship to God.

Jesus asks, "Who do you say that I am?" Have you answered this question for yourself? Have you fully embraced Jesus and who He claims to be? What I'm *not* asking is: Did you pray a prayer to receive Jesus when you were little? Or do you go to church on a regular basis? Or do you believe in God? Or do you read your Bible? You can do all those things and still not have a life that reflects the truth of who Jesus is. Maybe you have known Jesus but sometimes failed to believe Him when He declared who He is. So many times in this modern church culture we can come up with our own brand of Christianity. We seek to have the life we want, to attain the goals in life we want

---

[8] "Why We Must Think Rightly About God." *The Knowledge of the Holy: the Attributes of God: Their Meaning in the Christian Life,* by A. W. Tozer, Harper-SanFrancisco, 1992, p. 1.

to accomplish, and to fulfill our dreams, and we simply just add Jesus to it all. Jesus becomes a part of our life, but fails to be all of our life. We know a lot about Jesus, and live life for ourselves. This should not be. This is not gospel-centered living, this is not worship, this is not Christianity. Search your heart today. Do you know Jesus? Are you able to answer His question that's given to Peter in this moment? If we truly knew who Jesus was and believed these truths, what would our lives look like? Over the next seven days we'll go on a journey to take a closer look at the character of Jesus and allow these truths to fuel our worship and change our lives.

"How we treasure all Thy names, Lord,
How much they to us unfold;
All their worth and all their sweetness
We in love will ever hold.
Precious Savior, we adore Thee,
Worship unto Thee we bring;
Our Emmanuel, we exalt Thee,
And Thy praise will ever sing."
Joseph P. Holbrook

DAY 21

I AM THE BREAD OF LIFE

> *"And Jesus said to them, 'I am the bread of life. He who comes to Me shall never hunger, and he who believes in Me shall never thirst.'"* **–John 6:35**

Jesus here, after feeding the 5,000 with five loaves and two fish, was speaking to the people who were full with the food that was provided. They were seeking more signs and saying that if Jesus provided them more of these signs, they would believe in Him. Jesus tells them about a bread that comes from heaven, and the people desperately request this bread from Jesus. That's when He boldly declares, "I AM the bread of life." Jesus reveals truth about Himself in this moment. He not only reveals His deity, displaying the fact that He is God to those around Him, but He is communicating that He alone is where true satisfaction and fulfillment is found.

Every human has a need for a physical hunger and a physical thirst. What's even more important to God is the deep spiritual hunger that lies within each person. A result of the fall of man from the very beginning was the need to be deeply satisfied in the soul. The problem comes when we seek to live independently from God. We run to everyone and everything else to satisfy this deep hunger and deep thirst. Jesus is revealing to these people and to us right now today, that He is not just a way to find fulfillment or satisfaction for life, He is the life and satisfaction we need. What if we, as worshipers of God, truly believed this truth about Christ? How would we then live? If we believe Jesus is the bread of life, we will look to Him moment by moment, in the midst of all the distractions in this world that fight for our affections. We run to various pleasures to find satisfaction, and even though they may not be inherently sinful things, they take the place of God and we fail to enjoy Him. We run to empty wells to quench our thirst; we stay there and are left unsatisfied. When the temptation comes to run to other things for ultimate pleasure and enjoyment, we need to call to mind the truth of Jesus— that He alone is the source of all sustenance and satisfaction. Jesus is the bread that came down from heaven, and He shed His own blood on a cross and rose again from the grave to rescue us from these false pleasures that will only leave us empty. The gospel proves that Jesus has the position and power to be the only one to satisfy our longings. By faith embrace this truth today.

"Thou art the Bread of Life,
O Lord, to me,
Thy holy Word the truth
That saveth me;
Give me to eat and live
With Thee above;
Teach me to love Thy truth,
For Thou art Love."
Mary Artemesia Lathbury

DAY 22

I AM THE LIGHT OF THE WORLD

> *"I am the light of the world. He who follows Me shall not walk in darkness, but have the light of life."* **–John 8:12**

Something that we all know as humans is that everyone has a need for light. If we have no light, we have no direction; we're lost. If we have no light, we are fearful. If we have no light, we get hurt. And the same is true spiritually. Since the darkness of sin entered the world, we need light to dispel the darkness and bring forgiveness, comfort, healing and restoration. Jesus is boldly declaring that He IS this light. Without Him as our light, there is no hope. He's not just a temporal light that flickers and dies out, He's not just a light that lights up one particular place. When Jesus says, "I am the light," He is saying, "I am an eternal light, an unchanging light, and a light to the whole world."

How do we respond to this truth about Jesus? Well, the next part of this verse gives the answer, "He who follows me…." If Jesus is light in the midst of a dark and hopeless world, then why would our response be anything less than to follow after Him? Following Jesus is our response to this light. What Jesus goes on to tell us is remarkable. He tells us that the result of following this light is that we will not have to walk in darkness, but we will have the light that leads to life. If we truly believe that Jesus is our light, then naturally we would follow Him consistently, allow His light to reveal the darkness in our hearts, and allow His light to lead us on to lives of holiness and greater intimacy with Christ!

Are you presently living and walking in darkness? Hiding unrepentant sin, hoping you'll get away with it? Then you are not walking with Jesus. If you continue to walk in darkness and not in the light, the enemies' hooks sink deeper and will pull you toward greater destruction. Take the way of escape and follow after Jesus! Be transparent with Him and others; confess your sin and allow God's light to transform you into the child of light that He has saved you to be! "For you were once darkness, but now you are light in the Lord. Walk as children of light" (Ephesians 5:8).

"I heard the voice of Jesus say,
'I am this dark world's Light;
Look unto Me, thy morn shall rise,
And all thy day be bright.
I looked to Jesus, and I found
In Him my Star, my Sun;
And in that Light of life I'll walk
Till trav'lling days are done."
Horatius Bonar

DAY 23

I AM THE DOOR

> *"I am the door. If anyone enters by Me, he will be saved, and will go in and out and find pasture."* **–John 10:9**

Sheep, when being taken care of, need a sheepfold. A sheepfold was an enclosed area that would keep sheep safe at night. It was guarded by a fence that had one opening, which was basically a door for them to enter in and out. This was something that provided the sheep with shelter, security, and safety. In this context, Jesus is making the point of how much He loves and cares for His people, and He uses the familiar illustration that every listener in that time would understand, of Him being the shepherd. His people representing the sheep, and the sheepfold as being the family of God where there is love and security. This is a radical statement that Jesus is declaring when He says, "I am the door." What Jesus is communicating is that to enter into the family of God doesn't happen by joining a church or entering some sort of religion. Christianity is a person, Jesus Christ!

Does it amaze you that Jesus is the true door that leads to true salvation? This means that we were once abiding in death, but when we entered *the door*, we received true life. We were once in bondage to sin, Satan, and this world, but when we entered the door, we received redemption, freedom, and salvation from the power of these chains. We had no power to change the course of our lives, but when we entered the door, we received the power to change and become a true worshiper of God; the person He created us to be. This should encourage us and even change the way we view other people in the body of Christ. If we truly believed that everyone in the church entered by the door that is Jesus, then we would not think of ourselves as higher than another. We wouldn't allow pride to consume us, because we recognize that we all entered through the same door. We did nothing to earn it or deserve it, we are all simply products of God's amazing grace! Let's continue to look unto Jesus as the door of salvation!

"Thou art the Shepherd and the door,
For us to leave the sheepfold,
By Thee we have full liberty
And share the pasture freehold."
Witness Lee

DAY 24

I AM THE GOOD SHEPHERD

> *"I am the good shepherd. The good shepherd gives His life for the sheep."* **–John 10:11**

Leadership has always been something that people struggle with throughout all of history. Some don't want to be led. They feel they can govern their own lives, and no one tells them what to do. Some don't agree with people who are in leadership, so they respond with immoral, rebellious behavior. Some in leadership positions are themselves immoral, simply leading people to their destruction rather than to a prosperous end. Jesus Christ here declares, "I am the good shepherd." He is the true and perfect leader that everyone longs for. He is a shepherd who is good—He guides His sheep, provides for His sheep, comforts His sheep, guards and protects His sheep. But the greatest way that Christ displays that He is a good shepherd, is through the love and humility He displayed by willingly laying down His life for the sheep. Christ willingly came to those who like sheep have gone astray, who have gone their own way, and He gave His own life to save them and become forever their good shepherd. A true leader displays love for people that is sacrificial and unconditional.

If we truly believe this truth about Jesus, it should affect our lives and our worship of God. David declares in Psalm 23, "The Lord is my shepherd," and because he knew his shepherd, he goes on to confidently say, "I shall not want." Or in other words, "I shall not lack anything good." Jesus alone is our leader, our shepherd who knows what we need and does all in our lives for our eternal good. If this is the case, then like David we should be able to confidently say from our hearts, "I shall not want." To know Christ as our shepherd assures our hearts that there is no one better. No one else to run to. No new or better level to attain to in life. His love is better than life; He is all we could ever need, or ever want!

"The King of love my Shepherd is,
Whose goodness faileth never;
I nothing lack if I am His,
And He is mine forever."
Henry Williams Baker

DAY 25

I AM THE RESURRECTION AND THE LIFE

"I am the resurrection and the life. He who believes in Me, though he may die, he shall live. And whoever lives and believes in Me shall never die. Do you believe this?" **–John 11:25-26**

It was a really sad day in the town of Bethany. Mary and Martha, good friends of Jesus, lost their brother, Lazarus, to a lethal illness. Many were gathered in Bethany, and an incredible amount of weeping and mourning over the loss of a dear brother, but also a dear friend, was taking place. Jesus knew that Lazarus was sick, but He showed up on the scenes later than what Mary and Martha thought was needed. I believe this timing was for a purpose; Jesus knew exactly what He was doing. Jesus chose in that moment to display God's power and speak hope into a hopeless situation. Jesus comes to the tomb where Lazarus was laid, He simply says the word, and Lazarus is awakened from his dead state. He then walks out of the tomb. The people rejoice and are amazed.

Before this amazing miracle takes place, Jesus lovingly looks at Martha while she is no doubt wrestling with God and wrestling with the problem of death. Jesus declares, "I am the resurrection and the life." Jesus points out the fact that in Him is not just true life in the present, but eternal life for the future. He displays this truth by being the only one who has come and physically died, and physically rose again from the grave. Jesus was trying to teach these women that yes, He cared about their brother; yes, He had compassion in the midst of their sorrow; and yes, He desired to heal their brother. But more importantly, that He not only can raise people from the dead, but He himself is the resurrection, and He proved it by defeating death once and for all through His resurrection. We as Christians need to remember this promise daily: Jesus Christ alone is the conqueror over death and the grave. We have the victory and power of the resurrection living in us; we are more than conquerors in Him. Remember this today, friend. In Christ we have life eternal, and even though our body may die, we will live forever. Don't forget, we're going to heaven! The question is: Do *you* believe this?

"The Lord is ris'n: with Him we also rose,
And in His grave see vanquished all our foes.
The Lord is ris'n: beyond the judgment land,
In Him, in resurrection-life we stand."
William Paton MacKay

DAY 26

I AM THE WAY, THE TRUTH, AND THE LIFE

> *"Thomas said to Him, 'Lord, we do not know where You are going, and how can we know the way?' Jesus said to him, 'I am the way, the truth, and the life. No one comes to the Father except through Me.'"* **–John 14:5-6**

This verse is extremely meaningful and powerful when you read it in its full context and understand the situation in which Jesus is speaking these words. The disciples have many reasons to be troubled and discouraged in their hearts. In this upper room discourse, in the final hours before Jesus goes to the cross, He explains to His disciples how He is going to be handed over to be killed, He is going to be betrayed, and His betrayer is among them as He speaks. He is going to be denied by His own disciples. It's in the midst of a time where the disciples could be losing heart and losing hope that Jesus starts off this chapter saying, "Let not your heart be troubled." But it's interesting to see how you can almost hear the worry in Thomas' voice here when he says, "How can we know the way?" Jesus provides the hope and the encouragement for Thomas' heart, and I believe for us today, when He says, "I am the way, the truth, and the life."

How should this truth about Jesus affect our worship of God? We should be thankful that Jesus doesn't just offer to show us *a* way, but He declares to be the way; the only way. He also shows us that He isn't just a way to find truth, but that He Himself is to be the truth. And in Him is true life to be found, now and forever. This should cause us to respond in such rest, knowing that in Christ we are no longer lost without direction, we are no longer governed by the lies of the world, and we no longer experience the sting of death caused by sin. And this should also invoke in us the act of continual praise, knowing that exclusively through Jesus, because He is our mediator, we have full access to the Father without anything holding us back. This shows us that it's not a man or a leader that leads us to the Father's presence, it's Jesus Christ alone. So come today "boldly to the throne of grace, that you may obtain mercy and find grace to help in time of need" (Hebrews 4:16).

"Thou also art the way of life,
Which unto glory leads us;
The way of Thy reality,
Which into vict'ry speeds us."
Witness Lee

DAY 27

I AM THE TRUE VINE

"I am the true vine, and My Father is the vinedresser." **–John 15:1**

In chapters 13 through 16 of the Gospel of John, Jesus is giving final words to His disciples before He goes to the cross to die. This is what is most commonly known as the "upper room discourse." And what is on Jesus' heart is to share that He is the true vine. In this chapter I believe the central truth being communicated about Jesus is that any and all life is found in Him. He is the source from which all true life will flow. He also says that His Father is the vinedresser and that we, His people, are branches. God continues His work in the life of His branches and tends to the garden continually so that the garden can display the beauty that He intends for it to have. There is a certain responsibility that we as branches have, and a process that needs to take place for us to become the people God has created us to be. A branch is nothing without the vine. In fact, the identity of the branch is the vine. A branch is in desperate need to be connected to the vine if any life is going to come from it. This is its responsibility.

How does this truth affect our lives and our worship of God? We need to recognize our desperate need as branches to be connected to the true vine, which is Jesus Christ. We are nothing without Him and can do nothing without Him. We need to daily recognize Him as our source of any and all fruit that will flow from our lives. And if Jesus is the true vine, then that means there are a lot of false vines out there. There are many other things in this world that we seek to find our satisfaction in; that we seek to place our identity in. Even if it's something good, it can still be an idol and a false vine. These false vines can do nothing for us.

Aren't you thankful that in Christ, the identity issue is taken care of? As we are abiding in Jesus, we will continually find our identity in the right place and will never cease from being satisfied. Abiding in Christ, the true vine, is the safest place to be in life. I challenge you today to identify those false vines in your life, the things you're continually trying to place your identity in and find satisfaction in. These things will only leave you empty, lead you down a path of being fruitless, and ultimately lead to your destruction. Repent of these things and look to Jesus once again as the true vine!

"Thou true life-giving Vine,
Let me Thy sweetness prove;
Renew my life with Thine,
Refresh my soul with love."
John Samuel Monsell

DAY 28

WHY WORSHIP? BECAUSE HE'S GOD

"I am the LORD, and there is no other; There is no God besides Me. I will gird you, though you have not known Me." **—Isaiah 45:5**

I remember my wife at one season in her life was babysitting a six-year-old little girl named Jane. This sweet blonde-haired little girl needed a reason for everything. After my wife said anything, Jane's follow-up question was always, "Why?" Over time it became just a little overbearing to keep on answering each *why* question. But to say the least, it was pretty cool to see the childlike dependency and the genuine desire to want to have the reason behind everything. Oftentimes, as Christians we can get lost in our practices, or perhaps in our tradition, and we forget why we do what we do for God. We fail to be able to answer the *why* question, and we then find ourselves going through the religious motions. We know God calls us to worship Him. We know that our first calling on this planet is to be those who know, love, worship, and experience God. But why should we worship God? We've looked at many reasons but to go deeper, let's look at some more that we see in the Scriptures.

This verse above I believe provides for us a simple, but foundational, reason. Because He is God, and there is no other. God has been teaching this truth to the world since the beginning of time. He proved He was God, and there was no other—through creation, His sovereign rule over His people, His power to save through the cross of Jesus, and the resurrection from the grave, etc. He has constantly proved this truth time and time again—that HE alone is God. There is no other. So to put it simply, we worship God because He's God. The world will constantly choose to ignore God, ignore His rule, ignore His power and ignore His existence, and set up other people, places, or things to be "God" in their life, only to find themselves coming up empty. And although the world, and even we as His people, will at times forsake this truth and set up other things in the place of God, that doesn't take away or diminish this reality. We, as the people of God, need to constantly be reminding ourselves of the truth that He alone is God, our Lord, our Creator, our King, and there is no other besides Him. There's no one on equal ground, no rival to Him, no one and nothing that compares to Him. He is God and our Lord now and forever more!

"High King of heaven my victory won,
May I reach heaven's joys,
O bright heav'n's Sun!
Heart of my own heart, whatever befall,
Still be my vision, O ruler of all."
Eleanor Hull

DAY 29

BECAUSE HE SAVED US

> *"This is a faithful saying and worthy of all acceptance, that Christ Jesus came into the world to save sinners, of whom I am chief. Now to the King eternal, immortal, invisible, to God who alone is wise, be honor and glory foreverand ever. Amen."*
> **–1 Timothy 1:15, 17**

For the apostle Paul, he possessed an awe for God that should inspire us, and that we can learn from. Awe is simply a mixture of amazement, wonder, and expectation which leads to adoration and worship. This is what Paul possessed, and is displayed in the verses above. Paul began to speak of and express the extravagant love of God that was lavished upon him, that even when he, being the self-proclaimed "chief of sinners," a former murderer of Christians, and a blasphemer, Christ still chose to lay down His life for him and save him. Christ had mercy on Paul. Paul knew what kind of a man he really was. This was unfathomable for Paul and when he began to think on this reality, he couldn't help but respond with amazement, wonder, adoration and praise. His adoration and praise didn't stop at his lips but carried over into his life.

Why do we worship God? Because He saved us. Paul's worship was evident. Is your response like Paul's? If it isn't, perhaps you've not thought about or meditated upon the great mercy that God has had on your soul. Maybe you've forgotten the great lengths that Jesus had gone to save and redeem your life. Maybe you've grown up in church or have been around churchy people and churchy things for so long that you've become so desensitized and numb to the reality that Jesus, the God who created all that we see, sees you, knows you, and loves you. Has the phrase "Jesus loves you" just become too simple for you? Just another thing that Sunday school teachers say? When you think about your salvation, are you moved to awe? Are you so amazed that it moves your heart to such deep wonder and gratitude that it results in deeper submission, devotion and praise? Search your heart today, friend. Take time to think upon all Christ has done and thank Him for it all.

"Because the sinless Savior died,
My sinful soul is counted free;
For God, the Just, is satisfied
To look on Him and pardon me;
Hallelujah! Hallelujah!
Praise the One,
Risen Son of God!"

C. L. Bancroft/Shane and Shane

DAY 30

BECAUSE HE REDEEMED US FROM SIN

> *"And Moses said to the people: 'Remember this day in which you went out of Egypt, out of the house of bondage; for by strength of hand the LORD brought you out of this place. No leavened bread shall be eaten."* **–Exodus 13:3**

Why do we worship God? Because He redeemed us from sin. The awe that we experience and the praise we express when we think on our salvation, like we talked about previously, doesn't just stop at our lips, but carries over into our lives. Our worship of God is manifested when we cease from pursuing sin and pursue Jesus. It's our reasonable response to His redemption. The fact of the matter is a heart truly redeemed by Jesus will naturally put off sin. In these verses, we see Moses giving a command to the people of Israel right after they were set free from their slavery in Egypt. This was a pretty huge deal. Countless days and months and years of being in bondage, and now finally they are free. Moses now shows them what their response must be as they take time to commemorate and remember this amazing victory the Lord brought forth: "No leavened bread shall be eaten." In essence God is saying, "Not even a hint of leaven is to be consumed."

Leaven, in Scripture, is oftentimes a picture of sin. The thing that represented sin was not to be consumed by the Israelites. Here is the issue; even though we are redeemed, so many times we don't live as if we're redeemed. This should not be! If we are ones who have been redeemed, purchased out of the slave market, then we should live as who we are! Not even a hint of sin should be dwelling in us; instead we should live lives of confession and repentance. One of the motivations the apostle Peter uses when he is exhorting the believers to live holy lives is "knowing that you were not redeemed with corruptible things, like silver or gold ... but with the precious blood of Christ, as of a lamb without blemish and without spot" (1 Peter 1:18-19). If you've been living a life that's been governed by sin, or there's sin that is besetting you, remember who you are, friend. Christ redeemed you at the cross, and there still remains redemption and forgiveness for you. Worship God by repenting and placing Him as the master passion of your life.

"Redeemed, redeemed,
Redeemed by the blood of the Lamb;
Redeemed, redeemed,
His child, and forever, I am."
Fanny Crosby

DAY 31

BECAUSE HE'S WORTHY

> *"You are worthy, O Lord, to receive glory and honor and power"*
> **–Revelation 4:11**

Something that characterizes our God and is incredibly vital to understand if we are to be worshipers of Him, is the fact that He is worthy. We worship God always because He is worthy. What does this mean? When someone who is an incredible athlete, or someone who displays excellence in some talent or ability, wins a competition because of that excellence, they receive a trophy or medal or a prize. What people are recognizing is that because of their skill and ability, they rightfully earned honor, and are fully deserving of it. Webster's dictionary defines this word *worthy* as "possessing worth or excellence of qualities; virtuous, estimable."[9] The English word *worthy* itself contains the word *worth*, which is appropriate because the God that we say we know, love and worship is a God of infinite worth. When we say we worship God because He's worthy, we're saying that God fully deserves all worth, glory, and honor ascribed to Him. Not only this, but what is different about God as opposed to an athlete who receives an award is that God is the only One deserving of honor, not just because of what He's done to earn it, but who He is in the first place. He has no one that comes close to Him; no one that could ever be some sort of competition against Him. He alone is worthy, and there is no other!

Knowing this simple truth should cause us, as people of God, to go past what we feel or what our flesh desires, and worship God every minute of every day. I will go as far as to say that as people of God, if we don't necessarily "feel" like worshiping God, we are just normal human beings. We won't always "feel" like worshiping God. Feelings are temporal, fleeting, and constantly changing. This is why we don't

---

[9] http://webstersdictionary1828.com/Dictionary/Worthy

worship God because we feel like it, we worship God because He's worthy! Through the pain, He's still worthy. Through the uncertainty of life, He's still worthy. Though we may not fully understand God's ways, He's still worthy. He always was, always is, and always will be. May we join with heaven and say with our lives, "You are worthy, oh Lord, to receive glory and honor and power."

"Jesus, Thou alone art worthy
Ceaseless praises to receive;
For Thy love and grace and goodness
Rise o'er all our thoughts conceive."
J. A. Trench

DAY 32

BECAUSE HE IS CREATOR

"For You created all things, and by Your will they exist and were created." **–Revelation 4:11**

The twenty-four elders before God in heaven go on to say, in the next part of this verse, one of the many reasons God is worthy of their worship, adoration, and praise. Because He is the Creator of all things. In the beginning, God was there. He is pre-existent, self-existent, and self-sufficient. God was in the beginning, and as the Bible tells us in Genesis 1:1, He created the heavens and the earth. God, by His great power and His word, breathed all of life into existence. Not only did He create the ground and the sky, the waters and the clouds, the mountains and the stars and planets, the beasts of the field and the birds of the air, but He created man; He created you and me.

One of the things that would cause our worship of God to be reasonable is the fact that He is our creator. In the very beginning, He breathed the breath of life into man, and he became a livings soul. That means that you and I today are the very creation of God. The Bible tells us that in Him we live and move and have our being (Acts 17:28). If this is true, and we know it is, shouldn't our response as the very creation of God, created in His image, and who have been redeemed by the blood of Jesus, be to give our life and everything we are to God for His glory? What if I told you that this is the very reason you were created by God in the first place? You were placed on the earth for many God-ordained purposes, but the main purpose was to worship and enjoy fellowship with God. He created you, friend. Don't forget it. It's His breath in your lungs. He has placed life within you, so worship Him by giving yourself fully to Him afresh today.

"All creatures of our God and King,
Lift up your voice and with us sing,
Alleluia, alleluia!"
William Draper

DAY 33

BECAUSE OF HIS GREAT LOVE

> *"But God demonstrates His own love toward us, in that while we were still sinners, Christ died for us."* **–Romans 5:8**

Have you stopped to think about the amazing love of God? Great theologian and author J.I. Packer said, "To know God's love is indeed heaven on earth."[10] God is a God who loves. Paul the apostle, in Ephesians chapter 3, prays for the church that they would come to a greater knowledge of God's love; to know the height, the depth, the width, the length of God's love. His love is incredible. It surpasses our human understanding and knowledge. In this verse above, we learn three things about God's love.

1. THE INITIATIVE OF GOD. "BUT GOD DEMONSTRATES HIS LOVE TOWARD ... "
Throughout scripture, what we notice about God is that He is always the initiator. He initiates the relationship He desires with man. God's love is an initiating love; a pursuing love. He didn't just say, "I love you," He demonstrated that love.

2. THE COMPASSION OF GOD. "IN THAT WHILE WE WERE STILL SINNERS,"
Aren't you glad the verse doesn't say, "while we were doing our best" or "while we were acing it every time"? No, it says God chooses to "demonstrate His love while we were yet sinners," while we were trapped and enslaved to sin. While we were spitting in God's face. While we were at our worst, God chose to show us His amazing love. He is such a compassionate God!

3. THE GIFT OF THE SON OF GOD. "CHRIST DIED FOR US."
How did He choose to demonstrate His love toward us? The greatest way possible; God sent His own Son, Jesus Christ, to die upon a cross. Jesus said this: "Greater love has no one than this, than to lay down one's life for his friends" (John 15:13). He did that for us at the cross.

---

[10] "The Love of God." *Knowing God,* by J. I. Packer, InterVarsity Press, 1993, p. 117.

He died the criminal's death we deserved, took our place, and at the same time took away our sins, was buried in a grave, and rose again three days later to not only prove that He was God, but to seal our forgiveness and our justification, and once and for all do away with sin and death.

Why do we worship God? Because He loves us. Think upon His love today and respond to Him in adoration and praise! His love for you is all you need!

"Man of sorrows!
What a name For the Son of God who came
Ruined sinners to reclaim,
Hallelujah!
What a Savior!"
P. P. Bliss

DAY 34

BECAUSE HE ROSE AGAIN

> *"But now Christ is risen from the dead, and has become the firstfruits of those who have fallen asleep. For since by man came death, by Man also came the resurrection from the dead."*
> **–1 Corinthians 15:20-21**

The truth on which hangs all Christianity is the resurrection of Jesus Christ from the dead. It's what proves that our faith is real, what proves that our Jesus was who He said He was, what secures our hope, and what makes our worship of God of any value. Why, or shall I say, how can we worship God? Because He is risen from the dead. The death of Christ is incredibly important. We rest our hope of forgiveness and atonement for sin on the death of Jesus upon the cross. But Jesus didn't just stay upon the cross and then lay in the tomb for the rest of eternity; three days later, He came back to life and rose again for our justification! One of the reasons that Jesus is worthy of our worship, and one of the reasons we should be responding to Him on a daily basis, is not just because He was our crucified Savior, but He's our risen Savior. He's forever in heaven seated high at the right hand of the throne of His Father reigning over all, and is coming back to set up His kingdom on earth.

So then, because our Savior is our resurrected Savior, because He is alive even now, the promise then is that Jesus, through the resurrection, is alive in you! The same power that raised Jesus from the dead lives inside of us, giving life to our bodies to live in the newness of life that He has promised us. So not only is the resurrection *why* we worship Him, but it's also *how* we are able to worship Him. Without His resurrection power, we cannot have any power to worship Him. Let's rely upon His resurrection power to worship Jesus today, friend. No amount of human strength can genuinely enable you to do so.

"Then bursting forth, in glorious day
Up from the grave He rose again!
And as He stands in victory,
Sin's curse has lost its grip on me,
For I am His and He is mine,
Bought with the precious blood of Christ!"
Stuart Townend

DAY 35
BECAUSE HE IS COMING AGAIN

> *"Finally, there is laid up for me the crown of righteousness, which the Lord, the righteous Judge, will give to me on that Day, and not to me only but also to all who have loved His appearing."* **–2 Timothy 4:8**

Something I love about the teaching of the apostle Paul is that he constantly lived in anticipation of, and drew peoples' attention to, the fact that Jesus is coming again for His church. This is considered the "blessed hope" of the church. Of course, we rest our hope in the death, burial, and resurrection of Jesus, but a huge part of the gospel is the fact that Jesus promised to come back to the earth and receive us to Himself, to be with Him for all eternity! (John 14:1-3) Why should we passionately pursue being true worshipers on this earth? Because Jesus is coming again! He's going to receive to Himself those who had saving faith in Him, and set up an eternal rule and reign upon the earth. All things will be made new! This should serve as great motivation for us, who call ourselves Christians, to live a life of true worship on the earth.

This is how the apostle Paul lived. He lived with great expectation that Jesus will return. Because of this, He lived a life of devotion and worship to God. He points out in this verse that as he is about to finish this great race and bring to a close this good fight he's been fighting, he's been striving for a crown that will be given to him when he finally meets his Savior. This crown is given to all those who "love His appearing." The question for you today is this: do you love His appearing? Do you long for it? Live in anticipation for it daily? If not, this could be why there is a lack of discipline in your life. A lack of passionate pursuit of Christ in your life. A lack of holiness in your life. Pray and ask God to work it in your heart to love His appearing. To worship God with your life passionately, knowing that He is coming soon. No one knows the time or the day. It could be today.

"And Lord, haste the day
When my faith shall be sight,
The clouds be rolled back as a scroll;
The trump shall resound,
And the Lord shall descend,
Even so, it is well with my soul!"
Horatio Spafford

DAY 36

SIMPLY HIS SERVANTS

> *"Let this mind be in you which was also in Christ Jesus, who, being in the form of God, did not consider it robbery to be equal with God, but made Himself of no reputation, taking the form of a bondservant, and coming in the likeness of men."*
> **–Philippians 2:5-7**

To be like Jesus is the highest and most extravagant goal for every believer. If we really desire to grow as worshipers of God, an area that we should strive to become more like Jesus is in the area of humility and service. If worship is our response, one of the ways we should respond to God is to cultivate a life of humbling ourselves before God, and humbly serving the needs of others. A servant is one who willingly lays down his own rights, wants, needs, and desires, to help meet the needs of another. This is exactly what Jesus displayed. Being a servant presupposes a greater authority, and a submission to carry out what is commanded. Being a servant implies that you are others-focused, and desire to sacrifice and do whatever it takes to attend to the needs of another. Jesus submitted to the authority of His heavenly Father, laid down His own rights and privileges, all for the purpose of meeting the great need of all mankind. He humbled Himself daily as a servant, and served you and me by going to a cross to take away the sin of the world. We look to Jesus for our example of servanthood.

I think what we soon come to find is that not only is being like Jesus a great goal and great blessing, it's also a great difficulty at times. The reason it is difficult is not because God makes Christlikeness burdensome, and makes His commands impossible to follow, it is because Christlikeness comes at a cost. And that cost is a moment by moment death that our natural human nature needs to die. What is natural is to allow our pride to rule, and to serve self; and yet the plea comes to us, "Let this mind be in you which was also in Christ Jesus." The key here is *let*. To have the very servant mindset of Christ is a work that God, by His grace and by His Spirit, wants to accomplish in our lives. We look to Jesus as our strength for servanthood. But we must simply "let" it happen. This one word implies a surrendering and a yielding that must take place. May we respond to God by allowing this servant mindset that Christ possessed to be in us. As individuals surrender afresh and anew to Christ in this way, we'll see God lead us into deeper intimacy with Him; we'll see greater fruit produced, and we'll see the work of the gospel be furthered. Maybe then we'll see revival take place.

"Worlds and men and angels
All consist in Thee,
Yet Thou camest to us
In humility."
Daniel Arthur McGregor

DAY 37

THE LIFE OF DISCIPLINE

"... and exercise yourself toward godliness. For bodily fitness profits a little, but godliness is profitable for all things."
–1 Timothy 4:7-8

When we seek to pursue after Christ and deepen our relationship, it's always necessary to remember that we've been saved from something, and also saved *to* something. We were saved from the life of slavery to a life lived in devotion to Christ. So, now daily and practically, we seek to put off the old life like an old garment, and continually clothe ourselves in the new life, like a new, clean garment. In doing this we live out Galatians 2:20 where I believe Paul clearly lays out what the Christian life is supposed to look like. And I believe it can be summed up in these five words, "No longer I ... but Christ." In order to do this, it's going to take Spirit-empowered, faith-filled, gospel-centered discipline.

Paul instructs Timothy to exercise himself spiritually, knowing that the purpose of this should be godliness. Physical exercise results in greater physical strength; spiritual exercise results in greater spiritual strength. Discipline is simply our response to God's goodness and grace to us. It's knowing that even though God is the one who ultimately accomplishes godliness in us, it takes our willingness and surrender to partner with Him in this pursuit of godliness. Are you taking this call to exercise yourself for the purpose of godliness seriously? To worship God with your life is a life of discipline. Today, ask God what disciplines are lacking in your life—Bible intake, prayer, journaling, worship, fellowship, etc.—and pray for fresh passion to exercise yourself in these ways for the purpose of godliness.

"'Consider Him,' and thus thy life shall be
Filled with self-sacrifice and purity;
God will work out in thee the pattern true,
And Christ's example ever keep in view."
Emily May Grimes

DAY 38

THE GOAL OF EVANGELISM

"Jesus said to her, 'Woman, believe Me, the hour is coming when you will neither on this mountain, nor in Jerusalem, worship the Father.'" **–John 4:21**

Jesus is on this tiring journey from Judea to Galilee, and the Bible tells us that He "needed" to go through Samaria. As He does, He chooses to sit with a woman; and He seeks to engage her heart and cause her to believe in Him as the Messiah. What's so interesting to note is that as Jesus is "evangelizing" to her, the topic of discussion that comes up is that of worship. I believe that's intentional and very much guided by Jesus, even though she's the one who brought it up. First, He points out her worship problem by revealing her dark past of immorality and idolatry. Then she brings up worship, and I believe Jesus had her in the perfect place to turn her from a woman who worshiped herself and other things, to a worshiper of God. Worship was the goal of evangelism.

This should be our goal as well. As we seek to preach the gospel to lost souls, which I believe every Christian should be doing, we need to understand that worship is our motivation. Not only should we seek to evangelize as an act of worship, we should also recognize that our goal for the person we evangelize to is worship as well. When we see the lost world around us, our hearts should break to see people worshiping themselves and others. When that takes place in someone's life, only destruction follows. Idols promise much, but never deliver or satisfy. Truly worshiping Jesus and pursuing a relationship with Him is what satisfies the longing soul. May we seek to preach the gospel to this world everywhere we go throughout each day, recognizing that as they receive the gospel, they will become true worshipers of God and live the abundant life Jesus promises. May this be what drives us to share the good news of Jesus!

"Saints, time is of the essence,
'Tis time for us to gain
The fruit unto the gospel,
The ripened golden grain.
Oh, let us not be slothful,
Rise up and seize the day!
Let not our hours be wasted,
His purpose more delayed."
Samuel Sebastian Wesley

DAY 39

WORSHIP NURTURED THROUGH INTIMACY

> *"But one thing is needed, and Mary has chosen that good part, which will not be taken away from her."* **–Luke 10:42**

There are many verses in Scripture that begin with the words "one thing." This is one of them. I love this. I love how simple, yet profound, these truths are and how much they transform the way we view our lives as worshipers of God. Focusing our minds on what truly matters to the Father. It's easy to focus on "one thing." *You give me many things to worry about, and I may not be able to handle it, but one thing, I think I can do that.* But this "one thing" Jesus is pointing out, as simple as it is, can be overlooked and missed so easily. It's the place of intimacy and closeness with Christ. Martha, in this passage, is distracted with many other things, but Mary chose the better part: closeness with Jesus, hearing His word. There are four things to recognize in this verse that I believe will help guide us into deeper intimacy with Christ; the one thing I believe He desires from us the most.

1. The focus. Jesus says "one thing." He turns Martha's attention to one singular focus, and the aim that we should have as we grow to be true worshipers of Christ. It's the idea of consistent closeness to Jesus.

2. The necessity. Jesus says this one thing is "needed." When the God of all the universe says something is a need, then we better pay attention. This place of intimacy and abiding in Jesus is an absolute need for each of our lives, for so many reasons.

3. The choice. The verse goes on to say that "Mary has *chosen* that good part." This was a choice for Mary, and each day, friend, it is a choice for you. It takes our choosing. Our willingness. Our surrender to prioritize this necessary place of intimacy with the Lord.

4. The promise. Jesus ends this verse with an amazing and comforting promise. "Which will not be taken away from her." Everything in this world will eventually be taken away from us; our possessions, our passions, and people we hold so closely. But one thing is for certain, our pursuit of and intimacy with Christ will never be taken away from us. For we know that as we take our last breath here and our first breath in heaven, the people of God will have unhindered intimacy and closeness and will worship Him for all eternity.

"While I draw this fleeting breath,
When mine eyes shall close in death,
When I soar to worlds unknown,
See Thee on Thy judgment throne,
Rock of Ages, cleft for me,
Let my hide myself in Thee."
Augustus Toplady

DAY 40

GOD THE HOLY SPIRIT

> *"And the saying pleased the whole multitude. And they chose Stephen, a man full of faith and the Holy Spirit."* **–Acts 6:5**

The God we worship is triune. He is a trinity, one God made up of three distinct persons. So, when we say we worship God, we worship Him in His fullness—Father, Son, Holy Spirit. It's an essential truth that the Holy Spirit is God. He is given to us by Christ, He indwells us at the very moment we receive salvation, and He enables our spirits to be worshipers of God. But not only is it important to know who the Holy Spirit is, but it is vitally important to understand that the Holy Spirit plays an incredibly important role in our sanctification and worship of God in the present. There were many things that characterized the disciples of Jesus in the early church, but one of the preeminent things was that they were dependent, empowered, and filled with the Holy Spirit. Men like Peter, John, and in the verse above, Stephen, all lived lives that displayed a surrender to the work of the Spirit; first in them, then that work was manifested through them.

To be all that God has called us to be in Christ, we need to surrender afresh and anew each day to the power of the Holy Spirit. God is so committed to us that He gives us the Holy Spirit to become more like Christ, and more of a worshiper of God. But He is so committed to this world around us that the Holy Spirit works through us to continue and accomplish the work of Jesus on the earth. Jesus has ascended and is no longer physically on the earth, but make no mistake, He will return again in physical form. Until then we remember this: the Holy Spirit of God does the work of God through the people of God. I challenge you to start each morning by yielding yourself fully to the Holy Spirit and depend on Him for any effectiveness for the gospel. Are you worn out? Trying and striving so hard in your own strength to move your life and growth forward? We desperately need His power. How do we receive this? It's simple; we ask. We humbly ask and by faith allow God's Spirit to accomplish what He desires in our life.

"Thou hast, by Thy Holy Spirit,
Made us holy unto Thee;
And our spirit, soul, and body
Wholly sanctified will be."
John B. Dykes

DAY 41

A HEART CONDITION

> *"These people draw near to Me with their mouth, and honor Me with their lips, but their heart is far from Me. And in vain they worship Me, teaching as doctrines the commandments of men."*
> **–Matthew 15:8-9**

When I read of the Pharisees, and the hypocrisy, legalism, and disobedience that's displayed, it breaks my heart. For a few reasons; first of all, when you see the burdens they placed on others when they themselves were not living up to their own standards, the works that they did just for the motive of being seen by others, and the lack of compassion and love for the sick and the poor, you can't help but see how far they were from pleasing God, and they didn't even know it. The second reason I'm grieved when I read of the Pharisees and religious leaders, and how much they missed the point, is that I know that same heart of the Pharisees is alive in me sometimes.

I see that same heart of self-seeking, pride, and disobedience. Something we need to constantly be reminded of, something that is mentioned over and over again in Scripture and cannot be understated, is the fact that what God cares about in our lives is the place that no one sees—the place of our hearts. The greatest challenge in our life besides the trials and temptations that come from without, is the wretchedness that comes from within. We can display outward signs of religion, good works, and worship, but if our hearts are far from God, it means nothing. God doesn't desire the outward signs of meaningless religion; He desires a broken heart over sin, a genuine desire for His will, and a willful surrender each day. We must be thankful that because of the death and resurrection of Christ, we have a new heart. And now through His power, we can live lives of true worship that comes from a genuine heart. Without Jesus being our rescuer, we would be forever lost. We need His mercy day after day to continually rescue our hearts that are so prone to wandering. And because we serve a faithful God, He will. Give your heart to Him today. Ask Him to cleanse it and realign it with His Heart.

"We would count all things loss,
but Jesus gain;
Our inward parts cry out for You to reign.
Worthy You are our heart to claim—
Come, engrave on us Your name,
We would love You, Jesus, more."
Unknown

DAY 42

COUNTERFEIT CHRISTIANITY

"A woman came to Him having an alabaster flask of very costly fragrant oil, and she poured it on His head as He sat at the table." **–Matthew 26:7**

This wonderful story of a woman from Bethany named Mary displays a life of pure and costly worship. A life of worship to God will always be costly, something that we as Christians can often forget. Especially in our comfortable culture, it can be easy to have a "Christianity" that is purely convenient and without any sacrifice involved. But when it comes down to it, what we can conclude according to the Scriptures is that Christianity that is divorced from passionate commitment and sacrifice is no Christianity at all. This is counterfeit Christianity; a fake Christianity that only deceives yourself. Bishop J. C. Ryle reminds us of a very biblical truth, "A religion that costs nothing is worth nothing. A cheap Christianity, without a cross, will prove in the end a useless Christianity, without a crown." [11] Jesus, of course, tells us that "If *anyone* desires to come after Me, let him deny himself, and take up his cross, and follow Me" (Matthew 16:24). Here are some principles from this story in front of us that I believe will help us discover if we have embraced a counterfeit Christianity, and also discover the secret of true sacrificial living.

1. SACRIFICIAL WORSHIP REVEALS THE DEPTH OF OUR DEVOTION TO CHRIST.

This woman, Mary, took a flask of incredibly expensive perfume, and completely poured it out on Jesus to express her worship. The cost of this perfume is 300 denarii! Still hasn't hit you? That's like taking a year's worth of paychecks and pouring it all into a bottle of perfume. When we're devoted to something or someone, we will always pour out time, resources, and money into them. This is a good moment to evaluate the sum total of your life and ask yourself if maybe you

---

[11] "The Cost" *Holiness: It's Nature, Hindrances, Difficulties and Roots*, by J.C. Ryle, Moody Publishers, 1816-1900, p. 144

have fallen into a simply convenient life, filled with half-heartedness, complacency, and apathy toward the things of God. Maybe you have left your first love (Revelation 2:4). Or maybe you've embraced a false Christianity altogether and do not know God. There is hope for you! You can repent and believe the gospel and be filled with the power to live this life for the glory of God.

2. SACRIFICIAL WORSHIP NEEDS TO BE IN LIGHT OF THE GOSPEL.

This is worth repeating. This woman knew the love of Jesus toward her, so this act was a pure response. Someone said, "Discipleship divorced from the gospel is moralism" (Unknown). If we seek to live sacrificially, without the gospel as our foundation, we miss the whole point. We become people who try to keep rules without heart change, and without pure motivation.

3. SACRIFICIAL WORSHIP IS WORTH IT BECAUSE OF WHAT WE'RE GAINING.

Mary knew it would be worth it because of what she gained: Christ Himself! She experienced pure enjoyment of simply pursuing Christ, that it was so easy for her to pour out this expensive oil. Oftentimes we can focus too much on the cost we're paying, and forget the treasure that we're gaining, which is simply Jesus; in this life and the next!

"No wound? No scar?
Yet, as the Master shall the servant be,
And pierced the feet that follow Me;
But whole?
Can he have followed far
Who has no wound nor scar?"
Amy Carmichael

DAY 43

LORD, TEACH US TO PRAY

Part 1

"In this manner, therefore, pray: Our Father in heaven, Hallowed be Your name." **–Matthew 6:9**

Prayer is one of the rawest forms of our worship and intimacy with God. Prayer, put simply, is to communicate and have conversation with God. And even this is a loving response to our great God! That through Jesus Christ, we can have such an intimate relationship with God, that we would actually talk with Him. If we truly understood how much of a privilege and opportunity this really is, we would commit to talking to our God on a moment-by-moment basis. Prayer brings great joy, peace, fulfillment, realignment, and effectiveness in the kingdom of God.

I love how Jesus teaches His disciples, and us, to pray. I specifically love how He starts, and I believe sets in our minds as believers the proper perspective of prayer which is this: prayer should always be approached with an attitude of reverence and worship. This is the foundation of lifelong effective prayer. He starts with "hallowed be your name," or in other words, "Holy is Your name" or "may Your name be revered." It's your approach to God in prayer by ascribing worth, honor, and adoration to all that God is. Is this some kind of formula or step-by-step plan to prayer? No, I don't believe that's what Jesus is getting at. It's simply coming down to the heart attitude when we come to God in prayer. Today, begin praying not by jumping straight to requests, but with praise. Oh, that we would be people of constant adoration, and ascribe worth to His name because He is the God of infinite worth!

"I hasten to the place Where God my Savior shows His face,
And gladly take my station there,
And wait for thee, sweet hour of prayer!"
W. W. Walford

DAY 44

LORD, TEACH US TO PRAY
Part 2

> *"Your kingdom come, Your will be done on earth As it is in heaven."* **–Matthew 6:10**

Jesus continues to teach us how to pray and points out one of the most essential elements of prayer leads to deeper worship for the glory of God. It's this idea of being kingdom-minded; learning what it means to live in God's kingdom. What is God's kingdom? Well, that is a broad question with a variety of deep answers. To keep things simple, think of God's kingdom, as seen in this verse, with a twofold meaning. First, it's the present reality that I as a Christian live in now. Secondly, it is a future reality that we as Christians look forward to. I live in the kingdom of God today. Jesus came to earth not to manufacture a new religion with a new set of rules. He didn't come to just heal sick people, teach moral values, and draw crowds. Jesus Christ came to earth to establish a kingdom, and to do it His way. He established in the world His rule and reign, not by compulsion, conquering, and killing, but to suffer and serve; to deliver and to die. It's not a physical kingdom, but a spiritual one, where because of Christ's accomplishment on the cross, we are now able to give Jesus His rightful rule as King in our lives. There's a changed heart, a new mindset, where we now live with a commitment and passion to see God's will accomplished on the earth and see as many come to live in this kingdom as possible. Christ died and rose again for this end: that He would be Lord of both the living and the dead.

Not only are we living in God's kingdom now, but we as Christ followers live for the eternal heavenly kingdom not made with hands. A kingdom where Christ rules for eternity, only righteousness dwells, sin is no more, and we worship God forever! As we seek to pray, may we have this in focus. To be seeking first the kingdom of God (Matthew 6:33). We pray not so that we get our will accomplished in heaven, but to have God's will accomplished on the earth. May we seek to realign our will with God's and submit to His desires. It's only then that we'll see growth in our knowledge of Jesus, and God can use us powerfully to expand His kingdom. May the hope of His kingdom cause us to worship Him, not as religious people but as citizens of heaven!

"Let goods and kindred go,
This mortal life also;
The body they may kill:
God's truth abideth still;
His kingdom is forever."
Martin Luther

DAY 45

LORD, TEACH US TO PRAY
Part 3

"Give us this day our daily bread." **–Matthew 6:11**

Jesus is teaching us, His people, that God is trustworthy and a faithful provider. If this is true, then we can have the faith to respond to God by asking of Him what we need and desire. Something we need to remind ourselves of daily is that our God provides always. The apostle Paul reminds us of this truth, "And my God shall provide all your need according to His riches in glory by Christ Jesus" (Philippians 4:19). We have daily needs, spiritual and physical. We have a daily need for Jesus, who is *the* bread who comes down from heaven. He alone is our sustainer and all we need. And of course, we have daily physical needs. God cares enough to feed the birds of the air, and there is no doubt that He will feed us.

The Scriptures also teach us that God gives us what we desire. Jesus tells us in John 15:7 "If you abide in Me, and My words abide in you, you will ask what you desire, and it shall be done for you." Does this mean we can ask God anything and He gives us whatever we want? No. But as we are submitted to Christ, becoming a true worshiper of Him, our hearts become aligned with His, and He places within us His desires! God desires to provide for us and desires to bless us, but He desires that we ask. It's not wrong to ask God to do something! Of course, it should be in accordance with His will and not to serve self, but we oftentimes fail to ask. Do you limit God by how you pray? How you pray reveals whether or not you believe God is able. God desires that we keep asking, keep seeking, and keep knocking, but we often don't. Why? Perhaps we don't believe who God says He is. We don't take Him at His word. Maybe we have forgotten that God provided for the greatest need we could ever have by sending His Son to die; to pay for our sin when we could not provide the payment ourselves. Why would we not ask for provision for the lesser needs we may have? Today, ask God to help your unbelief. Remember that God is a provider. And the amazing part is, as Paul reveals to us in the verse above, God provides for His glory. God provides so that He may be glorified on the earth. So, pray. Ask. Believe that He can do "exceedingly abundantly above all that we ask or think, according to the power that works in us" (Ephesians 3:20).

"Great is Thy faithfulness!
Great is Thy faithfulness!
Morning by morning new mercies I see;
All I have needed Thy hand hath provided—
Great is Thy faithfulness, Lord, unto me!"
Thomas Obediah Chrisholm

DAY 46

LORD, TEACH US TO PRAY
Part 4

> *"And forgive us our debts, as we forgive our debtors."*
> **–Matthew 6:12**

Jesus is teaching us confession of our sin to the Father, and to forgive the sins of others. This should be a part of our daily times of prayer. This is so important to God. It's impossible to grow as a worshiper of God if we keep sin hidden and unconfessed in our lives. Of course, we are so thankful for God's love and grace, that He covers all our sin past, present and future based solely upon the blood of Jesus Christ on the cross. We are made perfect in God's eyes through Christ's work, but because of this fallen world, we still sin, and sin still separates. Sin separates and hinders our fellowship with God. God doesn't just desire our songs and sacrifices; He desires a broken heart over our sin. We can know for sure that as we daily confess our sin and repent, God is faithful to always forgive and give us the strength to turn from sin (1 John 1:9). No matter what you've done this week, or in the last month, or what you will do in the future, God's forgiveness runs as a never-ending stream for us to daily run to, and we will be restored and brought back. This is such amazing assurance for the Christian.

In light of this, we have the next part which is what we usually have the biggest issue with: *as we forgive our debtors.* This is the reasonable response of someone who has been forgiven: we forgive others. Do you have a debtor? Someone you hate? Someone you feel like you can't and won't forgive? As soon as you read these words, perhaps you thought of a person who's greatly hurt you or your family. I'll assure you of this truth: *you can't* forgive them. It's not natural for us to forgive. But the beautiful thing is that Christ *through you* ***can*** forgive that person. As you choose to pray for this person each day and ask God for a heart to forgive, I can promise you two things: 1) You will experience God's joy and be able to walk free of bondage to bitterness. Bitterness will hinder you from becoming all that you can be in Christ. And 2) You will glorify God and display the gospel. As you choose to forgive, what happens is you shine light on to the cross of Jesus Christ, and point people's attention to the forgiveness and freedom that He offers, and God is glorified in the world around you. You've been forgiven; therefore, forgive today, friend. Walk in the freedom Christ can give.

"Thy foes did hate, despise, revile,
Thy friends unfaithful prove;
Unwearied in forgiveness still,
Thy heart could only love!"
Edward Denny

DAY 47

LORD, TEACH US TO PRAY
Part 5

> *"And do not lead us into temptation, but deliver us from the evil one."* **–Matthew 6:13**

God is known as our great "deliverer." He delivered Noah from the flood, the Israelites from slavery in Egypt, the kings of Israel from their enemies, and David from the hand of Saul. This points to the fact that God has delivered all of mankind from the penalty, power, and someday, the presence of sin itself. But in this everyday battle that we face, God is faithful to deliver us from the enemies of our souls. Each day we are faced with the world which is competing for our affections; the devil who lies to us, accuses us, and tries to destroy us; and our flesh which tries to steer our lives in opposition to God and His Word. God can deliver and He *does* deliver. Although God doesn't lead us into temptation to sin, He does *test* us which is another translation of this word "temptation." Jesus is teaching that we can pray to not be led into great testing, even though testing is inevitable in the life of the believer.

In the face of every temptation is always a way of escape (1 Corinthians 10:13). Jesus Christ Himself is our way of escape from the evil one. God has made Christ's deliverance out of everyday temptation so available and accessible to us. We have to choose Jesus. That's why to resist temptation is an act of worship and faith, because by saying no to temptation, you are saying, "I know that Jesus and His love is eternally better and more satisfying than what this world and Satan is offering, and what my sinful nature is craving." When you pursue after Jesus and meditate on the truth of who He is and what He has done for you, you recognize that He has made you a new person, so the old life has no grip on you. You realize that He has freed you from the bondage of sin; so therefore it has no power over you, only the power that you give to it. And finally, you learn that Satan's lies don't stand against the truth of God's word. So today as you respond to God through prayer, pray for deliverance from temptation. Pray for deliverance from the schemes of the devil and walk in the victory that's already been won for you at the cross of Calvary!

"I need Thee every hour,
Stay Thou near by;
Temptations lose their power
When Thou art nigh."
Annie Sherwood Hawks

DAY 48

GOD, DID YOU SAY SOMETHING?

> *"Now the LORD came and stood and called as at other times, 'Samuel! Samuel!' And Samuel answered, 'Speak, for Your servant hears.'"* **–1 Samuel 3:10**

We can be so good at recognizing voices. When my dad or mom calls out to me from across the parking lot, even though I don't see them, I know their voice. A huge part of having conversation with God through prayer is that it is not just a one-sided conversation that we're engaged in. One of the things I find so amazing about my relationship with God is that He speaks to His children. But our problem is that we don't always hear His voice or even pay attention when He speaks. His will for you and me is that we hear His voice and learn to recognize it more and more so that we can know Him more and more. Jesus even said, "My sheep hear My voice, and I know them, and they follow Me" (John 10:27). And in this passage in 1 Samuel, Samuel is just a young boy serving the Lord in the house of Eli, the priest. One night God calls out three times to Samuel in his bed, and Samuel kept thinking that it was Eli calling him; he didn't recognize the voice of God at all! But after the third time Samuel is called, Eli tells him to go back to bed, and when he heard God's voice again, to say, "Speak, Lord, for your servant hears." Samuel hears the voice of God, surrenders to what God says, becomes a prophet, and is used to impact the world! Here are a few things we learn from this passage that will guide us in to listening for God's voice in our own lives.

1. GOD IS ALWAYS SPEAKING.

God was calling out to Samuel three times, but the problem was Samuel just wasn't listening. We have the full Bible— all sixty-six books! It's God's Word! He's always speaking. You most likely won't hear His voice audibly or out loud but you'll hear it through daily reading God's Word, the Bible!

2. YOU MUST BE LISTENING AND PAYING ATTENTION.

God is always speaking but oftentimes, we're just not listening. When you hear God's Word taught in church, or when you read it on your own, make sure you are listening!

3. BE READY TO SUBMIT AND OBEY GODS VOICE.

When Samuel finally heard God's voice, he prayed, "Speak, for *Your servant* hears." Do you have this attitude? When we hear God's voice, let's be ready to surrender and obey what He says.

4. BE READY TO BE CHANGED.

The best life is a life submitted to God, hearing His voice and obeying. God revealed Himself so powerfully through Samuel's life because he was submitted to God's voice. He was used to change a nation. As you hear and obey God's voice, you will see God change the whole course of your life for His glory, and the good of others!

"Lord, speak thy Word, upon us breathe;
Behold, dry bones fill all the earth
In graves and scattered 'round in death;
Lord, speak and breathe upon us!"
Witness Lee

DAY 49

CONCLUDING THAT GOD...

"Concluding that God was able to raise him up, even from the dead, from which he also received him in a figurative sense."
–Hebrews 11:19

We make conclusions about situations in our lives all the time, don't we? When circumstances become incredibly difficult, when life throws something our way that we weren't expecting, and the season becomes increasingly dark, our default reaction, even for those who know Jesus, is to think the worst. A trial or difficulty comes, and we automatically will have a conclusion made up in our mind of what the outcome is going to be, and it's usually life-shattering. In the life of Abraham, a great man of faith, a circumstance and test were thrown at him like he's never seen before. Hebrews 11 zooms in to a few situations in Abraham's journey, but what is said about his moment on Mount Moriah with Isaac is pretty amazing. In it we see a conclusion Abraham makes about God. When Abraham was faced with a command from God that seemingly contradicted the promise of God, he responded in a way that glorified God. He responded with obedience through difficulty and confidence through uncertainty. What we learn is how important it is to view our testings through the lens of God's unchanging character and God's glorious gospel. Doing this will not only keep us steadfast in the midst of trials, but will also allow God's light to shine from our lives and display His greatness!

When God's command came to Abraham to carry out the sacrifice of his own son, it says that he was going to follow through with it. He had every intention to. But here's the key: "Concluding that God was able to raise him up ..." He factored God into the difficult equation. How crazy is this? He had full confidence that God would raise up his son from the dead. The hope of the resurrection God can bring was Abraham's comfort and assurance. This was a conclusion before the conclusion. He was forced to have a confidence in that which was unseen, which is exactly what faith is, right? It is the "substance of things hoped for, the evidence of things *not seen*" (Hebrews 11:1). Of course, we know God stopped Abraham. He passed the test, and God reveals to Abraham that all along He Himself will provide the sacrifice. But we learn an incredible lesson of faith through this story of Abraham. May we be those worshipers of God who daily place our faith in our faithful God. May we look to His unchanging character and the power of His gospel and conclude that God is able. Do you believe this? In your present situation, what's been your conclusion? Look up, friend. Conclude that God is able; because He is.

"Faith sees the invisible,
Believes the incredible,
And receives the impossible."
Corrie Ten Boom

DAY 50

DOERS

"But be doers of the word, and not hearers only, deceiving yourselves." **–James 1:22**

What an amazing privilege and opportunity we have as people of God to have the word of God. The Bible is the most unique and marvelous book ever given to mankind. It's a book that comforts, a book that makes one wise, a book that builds up, a book that instructs, but most of all, it's a book that has an unfolding story of love and redemption woven through each chapter and page. God has chosen to reveal His character and His plan of salvation to us, and He uses the Scriptures to do just that. How are we to respond to this amazing revelation? One word: obedience. We've talked about before how worship of God is a posture of submission in the heart, and that heart overflows into obedience. Time and time again we see through the Scriptures that it's not enough to just read or hear, but we must practice and obey. This is where the blessing is truly found. I believe James gives us some steps to follow and take to heart, if we desire to be effective doers of God's Word for His glory.

1. THERE IS PREPARATION TO BE DONE.

James starts this passage in v. 21 with, "Therefore lay aside all filthiness and overflow of wickedness, and receive with meekness the implanted word." In order to truly be a doer of God's Word, we must first allow God to prepare our hearts. We need to lay aside the sin that is in our lives that is so filthy in the eyes of God, and begin to receive the Word of God. Just as when you're about to plant something beautiful you have to pull out the weeds and prepare the soil first, so too our hearts need preparation to receive the beautiful seed of the Scriptures.

2. THERE IS DECEPTION TO AVOID.

James points out that it's pure deception to think that just hearing or reading the Word of God is going to produce true lasting change if we never do anything about it. It can be so easy to hear and read, and it never affects our hearts. Just like the man who looks in the mirror, observes what's wrong, and never makes any change. That's why Paul exhorts us to "let the word of Christ dwell in us richly" (Colossians 3:16). God wants to change us, and when the Word of God dwells in us, it produces within us a heart of worship overflowing into obedience to Christ!

3. THERE IS A REWARD TO RECEIVE.

We learn going further in this passage that being a doer of God's Word is the most rewarding thing we can ever do. As we daily practically apply God's Word, James says, "This one will be blessed in what He does" (James 1:25).

4. THERE IS A GIFT TO SHARE.

As we are doers of God's Word and are people of obedience, naturally fruit is produced that will build up others. Here James specifically refers to visiting orphans and widows as a practical way that would reveal God's work within our lives, but I believe this can apply to a variety of different areas as well. We must allow God's Word to overflow into the lives of those around us. In the Scriptures we have the eternal life-giving message of the gospel that has the power to save the sinner and sanctify the saint. May we first allow it to change us, then allow it to transform the world around us!

"Can you?
Then beloved,
Christ just waits for you;
Listen for His orders,
Glad His will to do;
Then when soldiers muster
At the set of sun,
And your name is mentioned,
Christ will say,
'Well done.'"
Margaret E. Barber

DAY 51

PURE DELIGHT IN OUR PRAISE

> *"From the rising of the sun to its going down the LORD's name is to be praised."* **–Psalm 113:3**

The psalmist here is declaring that praise to the name of God is a response that should be happening all day every day! One of the reasons that praise is reasonable is this simple fact: praise is commanded by God. This is an interesting thought. No other being demands praise except God alone. Of course, knowing who God is and what He has done are definitely things that will cause us to naturally praise Him each day, and should be enough to invoke our praise. But I believe there is another foundational aspect to praise that should be recognized and understood. If any other person commanded us to praise them, we would find that rather strange and downright egotistical! Yet God commands praise, and we would never say that He is egotistical. One thing that God is after is the joy that His people can experience in Him. David declares in Psalm 16:11, "In Your presence is fullness of joy; at Your right hand are pleasures forevermore," and in another place, "*Delight* yourself also in the LORD" (Psalm 37:4). God's heart is that we simply enjoy Him forever! So here's a simple truth to consider: To praise God is not just expressing our enjoyment, but the act of praising God is to enjoy God.

C. S. Lewis writes in his book, *Reflections on the Psalms*, "I think we delight to praise what we enjoy because the praise not merely expresses but completes the enjoyment; it is its appointed consummation."[12] When God commands us to praise, what He desires for us is to experience the fullness of joy that comes by knowing Him, so He desires us to praise *Him* because there's nothing and no one greater or higher than Him! Have you been experiencing a lack of enjoyment in your relationship with God? What I believe will allow you to find ultimate pleasure

---

[12] "Reflections on the Psalms." *Reflections on the Psalms*, by C. S. Lewis, sHarperOne, an Imprint of HarperCollinsPublishers, 2017, p. 81.

in God is if you commit to making praise a habit. That from the rising of the sun until it goes down, you would praise the name of Jesus!

"Come thou Fount of every blessing,
tune my heart to sing Thy grace.
Streams of mercy never ceasing,
Call for songs of loudest praise."
Robert Robinson

DAY 52

PRAISE FOR GOD'S GREATNESS

> *"Great is the LORD, and greatly to be praised; and His greatness is unsearchable."* **–Psalm 145:3**

God's greatness should always evoke our praise. We praise God because He is deserving of praise, and one of the reasons He is deserving of praise is that He is great! In other words, God is big, He is elevated, He is majestic and deserves to be magnified in the hearts and minds of every person. He created all things and He is before all things; there never was and never will be anyone like Him. We have to remember that at the foundation of our praise to God is the greatness of God. All throughout Scripture, we read of God's greatness, and the awe and praise that's expressed by the Scripture writers. We read, "The LORD reigns, He is robed in majesty" (Psalm 93:1), and "For the LORD is the great God, and the great King above all gods. In His hand are the deep places of the earth; the heights of the hills are His also (Psalm 95:3-4). It's the knowledge that He is great that begins to fuel praise from the depths of our hearts.

When we know God's unsearchable greatness, we recognize that He is the only one deserving of reverence and awe. We recognize that He is stronger than my circumstances appear to be. We recognize that our trust belongs to Him and Him alone. When we finally come to some understanding of God's greatness and what it does to our lives, it's then that we come to understand that our praise is reasonable. Today, begin to set your mind upon the greatness of our God. If in your own mind you've begun to limit God and make Him small in your thinking, in light of your current circumstances, repent of that and reestablish right thoughts about who Your God is. Live a daily life of praise to God for His greatness!

"Great is the Lord,
and greatly to be praised,
In the city of our God,
In the mountain of His holiness.
Beautiful in elevation,
the joy of the whole earth,
Is Mount Zion,
on the sides of the north,
The city of the great King."
Unknown

DAY 53

OVERFLOWING PRAISE

> *"My heart is overflowing with a good theme; I recite my composition concerning the King; my tongue is the pen of a ready writer."* **–Psalm 45:1**

Praise is never something that we conjure up or manufacture within us; praise is always the overflow of a heart changed by God. I love how the psalmist declares that he is filled with a good theme and it is overflowing. When a cup of water overflows, the water coming off the sides of the cup is not something manufactured by the cup itself. It's simply a natural result of so much water being poured into the cup by an outside source. Also, when a cup overflows, the water affects everything else around it. Similarly when we have a theme filling our hearts, it naturally overflows and impacts and influences the lives of those around us.

How do we continually allow praise to overflow from each of our lives? First of all, we need to know our "good theme." There's no greater theme than the redeeming love of God, displayed through Jesus Christ. The gospel should continually be our theme and meditation. The way that this is found and the way we go deeper into this theme is to continually study and meditate on the Scriptures. The entirety of the Scriptures has been given; God's Word, which is God's revelation of His love to all of mankind! It's important for every follower and worshiper of Jesus Christ to make it their aim to read through and study all of what God has revealed; the entirety of the Bible from beginning to end. It is when we do this that this good theme will continue to make its way deep into our hearts, and God's authority will become more established over our lives and we'll naturally live a constant life of praise. Secondly, we must remove the lid and allow the water to overflow. This should be a natural by-product, but we can so often hinder this work. This "good theme" should never be kept in, but should constantly be overflowing. We must yield ourselves to the Lord and continually seek opportunities with the people around us to speak the Word of God into their lives and be used by Christ to bring lasting impact! Who do you need to preach the gospel to this week? Who do you need to encourage in the body of Christ this week? Keep the Word of God coming in, and let your tongue be the pen of a *ready* writer.

"E'er since by faith I saw the stream
Thy flowing wounds supply,
Redeeming love has been my theme,
And shall be till I die:"
William Cowper

DAY 54

PRAISE IN MY DEPRESSION

"Why are you cast down, O my soul? And why are you disquieted within me? Hope in God; for I shall yet praise Him, the help of my countenance and my God." **–Psalm 42:11**

"For I shall *yet praise* Him." Is God still worthy of praise through depression? Through heavy and unwanted circumstances? The psalmist here is in a hard situation. He is pouring out his honest confession of hardship and brokenness to God. He indicates the fact that his tears have been his food day and night. He feels like God has forgotten him; he feels like his enemies are oppressing, and there is no hope in his current circumstance. And twice in this psalm he comes to the same conclusion; that through his pain God is the source of his hope and worthy of his praise.

We can so often feel the way the psalmist feels, but oftentimes we don't allow the same conclusion to take place in our hearts. What we desire is a change in circumstance. We desire to just have a "good day" again. We would never say it out loud, but we fool ourselves into thinking that just because we're "Christians" and "men and women of faith," that nothing difficult or tragic can ever happen to us. This then leads us to come to God and ask Him why, and secretly try to use Him to get what we want. And when we don't, we get up from our knees, shake our fist at God and allow anger and despondency to rule. Then ultimately, we become the object of our worship. All this does is lead to greater despair and even more difficultly. What God desires for us is for His presence to be enough, our identity to be secure in Him, and for us to worship Him through whatever we face! The psalmist concludes that even though he may feel the way he does, God is still the source of hope and worthy of praise, and that simply His presence is enough to help his countenance. He knows that he is God's possession and that God is his precious possession. God won't always answer the *why* question; He never promised to. He just wants us to praise Him for who He is no matter what He has allowed to take place. Are you a person of praise only when things are going well in your life? Or is your praise founded wholly in who God has revealed Himself to be, and His past faithfulness?

"One day they left Him alone in the garden,
One day He rested,
from suffering free;
Angels came down o'er His tomb to keep vigil;
Hope of the hopeless,
my Savior is He."
John Wilbur Chapman

DAY 55

QUIET MY SOUL

> *"LORD, my heart is not haughty, nor my eyes lofty. Neither do I concern myself with great matters, nor with things too profound for me. Surely I have calmed and quieted my soul."*
> **–Psalm 131:1-2**

David in this psalm displays such a simplicity with his life. He starts out by honestly admitting to the fact that he is currently not walking in pride, but he is displaying humility. He's not concerning himself with things too complicated, he's not thinking of himself too highly, but he's choosing to keep things simple. And what did this humility look like for David? This psalm seems to indicate that David was in a moment of solitude and silence, and in that moment, he chose to quiet and still his soul before God. Why does this show humility? Being still before God displays a dependence, hope and trust in God. It's a willingness to not be so stressed out with the busyness of life and take time to just be with God and meditate upon who He is. This is why David was known as a worshiper of God; a man that was after the heart of God.

Do you take the time to get away from busyness, stop the grand and important things you're involved with, and simply rest before God in silence? When we neglect this time of being still before God, this is actually pride in disguise. We can so busy ourselves up trying to prove that we are important. We believe that everything depends upon us, and our identity becomes wrapped up in what we do. Then our joy completely withers away. True humility is when we can learn to submit all of our lives to the Father and rest in Him enough to be able to quiet our souls. We will experience the fullness of joy that comes with being in His presence. If you feel like you don't have time to rest before God, you would do well to simplify your life. Jesus constantly pointed out to the disciples, even in the midst of busy ministry, that they need to get away to a lonely place and rest awhile (Mark 6:31). In other words, He wanted them to realize that they were not that important. The sooner we recognize that life and ministry do not depend upon us, the better. Jesus is a great example of this—constantly going away to rest with the Father. When was the last time you did this? A mentor of mine once said, "Take time to make time for the One who made time. If not, you'll be wasting your time."

"Jesus! I am resting, resting
In the joy of what Thou art;
I am finding out the greatness
Of Thy loving heart."
Jean Sophia Pigott

DAY 56

RIGHT RELATIONSHIPS

> *"Therefore, as the elect of God, holy and beloved, put on tender mercies, kindness, humility, meekness, longsuffering; bearing with one another, and forgiving one another, if anyone has a complaint against another; even as Christ forgave you, so you also must do."* **–Colossians 3:12-13**

Worship, of course, must always begin with my vertical response to God. But there is another aspect of my response to God which is when I love and serve other people. It's pretty significant that when asked, "What is the greatest commandment?" the second part of Jesus' answer is, "Love your neighbor as yourself. All the Law and the Prophets hang on these two commandments" (Matthew 22:36-40 NIV). Right before Jesus is going to the cross to be crucified for our sins, He prays for unity within the church; that they all would be one, just as the Father and He are one (John 17:21). Clearly, God's heart is for relationships to be right, that they may display His love to a world that so desperately needs it. God desires to receive just as much worship through our relationships with people as He does through our times of singing.

Unity in relationships is difficult; if it wasn't, the Bible wouldn't give us so much instruction on how to accomplish it. The apostle Paul, in these verses, lays out two beautiful ways we accomplish unity, and make sure our horizontal relationships are right. First of all, he points out who we are in Christ. "… as the elect of God, holy, and beloved …" If we don't know who we are and who we belong to, we will never be able to pursue unity in the relationships. Through the cross, Jesus Christ saved us and restored to us a right relationship with God resulting in a new identity. In Christ we are new creations! Fruitful horizontal relationships are always a by-product of my vertical relationship with Jesus. I need to recognize who God has saved me to be, pursue Him with all my heart, then I will begin to accomplish unity in my relationships, because now I'm not only viewing myself with this identity but now I am viewing others through this lens as well.

Secondly, he tells us to now put on those qualities that display genuine love and forgiveness. The root issue is changed, knowing who we are in Christ, and now the fruit can be changed, which is love. The way we display genuine love is by showing the same forgiveness that Christ showed, which takes being clothed in humility. To be quick to show forgiveness and grace when we are wronged is the quintessential heart of God. To withhold that grace and forgiveness is to forget how much grace and forgiveness Christ has shown to us.

If you have bitterness in your heart, and there is no unity between you and someone in the body of Christ, you have to check your relationship with Jesus. Are you living in light of who you really are? Do you view others in the body of Christ as a new creation, bought with Christ's precious blood? Have you forgotten how much you have been forgiven? If so, there is need for repentance and a change of heart so that you may worship Jesus once again by loving His church. Ask God today to give you His heart and passion to pursue unity, so that the church can have a oneness that glorifies God and fulfills our joy!

"Built up in love together,
Not one would criticize;
To perfect one another,
We all would exercise."
Witness Lee

DAY 57

BEING A BURDEN BEARER

> *"So it was, when I heard these words, that I sat down and wept, and mourned for many days; I was fasting and praying before the God of heaven."* **–Nehemiah 1:4**

You can't find a darker and more hurting place than Jerusalem at this point in history; not only physically but spiritually. All that's filling the air at this time is depression, disgrace, and distress. The walls of the city are broken, thrown down, and burnt with fire. Irreparable devastation. This Jewish man, Nehemiah, who is a cup-bearer to the king in Persia at this time, gets this horrible news about the state of the city—not only that but the state of his people's hearts also. There is a great need. After seeing the need, Nehemiah is moved with compassion, and is moved to prayer. He was a man dependent upon God, but also a man who was brokenhearted and burdened for the lives of people. He was a burden bearer.

How do you view people? Is there a burden and brokenness that leads you to action, all motivated by love? In Galatians 6:2, the Bible reminds us, "Bear one another's burdens, and so fulfill the law of Christ." What proves and displays our love for God is how we love other people. If we're really going to worship God with our relationships, we need to ask God for this heart. To see past ourselves and learn to be a burden bearer. When lives are hurting and broken around us, are we moved in our hearts? Are we able to sympathize with the hurts of others? Have we allowed our lives to be so bogged down with the cares and worries this world brings that we don't have time to even care at all? Does it bother us that there are countless people without Jesus dying each day? May these not be just boring statistics to us. May this reality grip our hearts and motivate us to show mercy, and to speak the Word of God, and allow the healing power of the gospel to turn the tide in the hearts of men! Pray today for a broken heart for people; the same burdened heart

Jesus had as He was moved with compassion to bear our sins on the cross, and now ever lives to be our high priest, and who continually sympathizes with our weaknesses!

"He giveth more grace
when the burdens grow greater,
He sendeth more strength
when the labors increase,
To added affliction
He addeth His mercy,
To multiplied trials,
His multiplied peace."
Annie Johnson Flint

DAY 58

THE SUFFICIENCY OF THE SON IN THE SCRIPTURES

"Then He said to them, 'O foolish ones, and slow of heart to believe in all that the prophets have spoken! Ought not the Christ to have suffered these things and to enter into His glory?' And beginning at Moses and all the Prophets, He expounded to them in all the Scriptures the things concerning Himself." **–Luke 24:25-27**

Jerusalem was a sad place for quite a few days. The man, Jesus, who was supposed to be the Christ, the Messiah, the Chosen One—who was supposed to overthrow the Roman rule and usher in His kingdom—has died. Everyone who believed in Him was walking in overwhelming despair. This chapter highlights two specific men who were walking down a road on their way to a village called Emmaus. A few of the people who followed Jesus, including His disciples, discovered an empty tomb early that morning and realized that Jesus was not there! No doubt these men were feeling the weight of what just happened. The risen Christ encounters these two men on the road, and these men don't know this, but this encounter will be something that completely changes their lives. When Jesus sees their downcast hearts and confusion, He lovingly rebukes these men, takes the Law and the Prophets, or what we would know as our Old Testament, and from beginning to end shows them Himself. Later, after their eyes were opened to the reality of who was speaking to them, they were amazed and reaffirmed to the disciples that He was who He said He was; that He was risen indeed.

Why were these two men "foolish" and "slow of heart to believe"? Because they did what you and I do oftentimes in our suffering—they believed a promise that God had never given. They were downcast because of a false belief in who Jesus truly was. They thought God promised a Messiah who would rule and reign and conquer the

Roman empire, and when all these events transpired, they despaired. We often fall into the same trap. We believe God promised us a Jesus that would give us whatever we want, a Jesus that wouldn't allow suffering to take place in our lives, or a Jesus that would answer all of our *why* questions. God sent us His Son to enter into our suffering. He took upon Himself our sins, died in our place, and rose again to be our great High Priest who we can totally relate with. That's why Jesus' solution to these men was to show them the reality of who He was through the whole of the Scriptures. Yes, God didn't promise an easy life with no pain, but what He did promise was to be our sufficiency. We need to believe in the sufficiency of the Son, and to do that, we run to the scriptures. A true worshiper of God responds to pain by running to the Scriptures to find the Son! Look to Jesus once again, friend. Like these men, allow Him to be sufficient for your heart's deepest struggles.

"I take Thee, Lord, to be my all.
Since all Thou art is mine;
I nothing have, and nothing am;
That nothing, Lord, is Thine.
Thou shalt be everything to me,
In all things my sufficiency."
Annie Wright Marston

DAY 59

DROPPING OUR GUARD

> *"Above all else, guard your heart, for everything you do flows from it."* **–Proverbs 4:23 (NIV)**

In any situation, if we will not stand on guard, we can and will get hurt. A mom can lose her little son if she fails to watch and guard him. A boxer can lose his fight if he carelessly drops his hands and lets down his guard. Where there are no guards, the enemy easily comes in. The same principle can be found true in our lives as worshipers of Jesus. All throughout Scripture, we can find story after story of good, God-fearing, strong men and women who fell asleep, let their guard down, and paid the price. To name a few: King David, resting instead of battling (2 Samuel 11); the disciples sleeping in the garden of Gethsemane (Luke 22:46); and King Solomon loving foreign women (1 Kings 11:1-3).

As I've said before, worship of God is less about what is seen outwardly, and more about what is going on in the place of the heart. What I love, where I find significance, what takes place in my devotion inwardly. It is so easy to let my guard down, get lazy, and allow the temporal pleasures of this world and the temptations of Satan to capture my affections. Why is it so easy? It's our nature. We are fallen creatures with hearts that are prone to wandering. Adam and Eve were created to be dependent creatures. They were perfectly dependent. But once they let their guard down and were tempted from without, their dependence upon God stopped, and they sinned. Even still now, we are supposed to be dependent. It's a constant mindset of knowing that I am simply a branch in desperate need of the True Vine. And when my heart is *not* guarded, when my heart is not in a place of continual surrender to my Savior, everything else in life will be affected.

I once heard Pastor Tedd Leavenworth preach a sermon and say these profound words, "Tomorrow's sins of commission are oftentimes a result of yesterday's sins of omission." The very next verses following

v. 23 in this proverb talk about the areas of life that are affected by not guarding our hearts. Our eyes, what we behold; our feet, where we choose to run to; and our lips, what we say. Now let's remember, in this pursuit of guarding our hearts, too much introspection is not a good thing either. We're called to be dependent but not *self*-dependent. If someone looked into the mirror without stopping, there would be something wrong. However, if someone never looked into the mirror, there would also be something wrong. We need to find the balance of resting in God's grace and trusting the enabling power of the Spirit, while also pursuing holiness and guarding our hearts. Today, ask God to enable you to guard your heart above all else. Examine your rotten fruit. It'll often point you to the corruption of the root. Run to God's grace and find that He is still your rescue.

"Let that grace,
Lord, like a fetter,
Bind my wand'ring heart to Thee.
Take my heart,
oh, take and seal it
With Thy Spirit from above."
Robert Robinson

DAY 60

THE ONE WHO IS SEATED UPON THE THRONE

> *"The twenty-four elders and the four living creatures fell down and worshiped God who sat on the throne, saying, 'Amen! Alleluia!'"* **–Revelation 19:4**

Worship is a broad subject. There are a lot of ways this word is defined, and there are a lot of ways it is expressed in our lives as Christians. We can explore the theology of this word, dive deeply into the Greek and Hebrew languages, and examine the cultural, musical way that we see this word used, but may we never lose the simplicity of what the Bible says about worship: There is a God in heaven, sitting upon an eternal throne, who forever deserves our worship. I love how at the end of this deep and action-packed book, the book of Revelation, the scene shifts to Christ. And in the midst of all of the world coming to an end, the wrath of God being poured out, and the new heavens and new earth being ushered in, we see God doing something. He is doing what He has always been doing; sitting upon His throne. Every being in heaven is falling to the ground and worshiping Him.

What needs to take place in every aspect of our lives, as Christian music artist and worship leader Matt Redman famously said, "We need to let the throne set the tone." May we never lose sight of the throne and Who is seated upon it. In the craziness of life, Christ is on His throne. In the depths of despair, Christ is on His throne. When life is smooth sailing, Christ is on His throne. He'll always be there with a vantage point that we don't have, and with the power to rule that we will never possess.

I'm ending this book with a starting point: As we pursue a life of worship, let this always be the foundation and beginning of our worship. As we continually gaze upon the throne, may our hearts always be in a "facedown" posture, because He gives us infinite reasons to do so. If this is our goal in all of life above all else, we will live lives that glorify Jesus Christ, build up the church, and further the work of the gospel in a lost and dying world!

"Crown Him with many crowns,
The Lamb upon His throne;
Hark! How the heav'nly anthem drowns
All music but its own!
Awake, my soul, and sing
Of Him who died for thee,
And hail Him as thy matchless King
Through all eternity."
Matthew Bridges

Made in the USA
Middletown, DE
24 July 2019